RIDIN'
The
MOUNTAIN

crusty boots

rusty spurs

dusty rawhide

Carol Shultz

GRIFFITH PUBLISHING CALDWELL, IDAHO

Printed in the United States of America

ISBN 0-9665240-1-2

Produced by Griffith Publishing
PO Box 247, Caldwell, Idaho 83606
208 459-0952

Ridin' The Mountain is a limited edition book
available while the supply lasts from the
author or publisher and selected outlets.

Events, names and places in this book are
based on personal experiences as recalled
by the author. Any errors of fact or omission
are totally unintentional.

Cover design by Linda Griffith Design
Front cover photo re-mastered by Cesar Soto,
   staff member, College of Technology,
   Andrews University, Berrien Springs, Michigan

Dedication

To Dave and Helen Bivens of the old Bar
Eleven outfit headquartered in the foothills
east of Payette, Idaho.

The adventures in this book and many more
that remain unwritten would not have been
possible without Dave's faith in two
schoolmarms working the cattle on
The Mountain.

Helen was the best chef on The Mountain.
You haven't eaten well until tying into her
steak barbecue with all the trimmings—at its
best topped off with her one-of-a-kind
cookies or rhubarb pie baked in the oven of
her wood-burning stove.

The generosity and support of Dave and
Helen through the years are greatly
appreciated.

Acknowledgement

This book would not have made it out the
door without the dedication and hard work of
Mary Odden, who spent countless hours
during more than one dark Alaska winter
transcribing fifteen or so audio tapes onto the
computer. She freely gave her time and
energy to this project. From the computer
disks and files Mary sent to us, this book
emerged.

CONTENTS

Foreword

by Mary Odden
Former Adrian High School Student

The stories you are about to read are true and are centered around one of the prettiest patches of rugged country you can imagine, known collectively as "The Mountain."

The woman who tells the stories and is their main character, Carol Shultz, is a friend of mine. I'm happy to say that now, because for most of my life my main feeling about "Miss Shultz" was that I didn't want her mad at me.

Carol probably won't swear at you, but she's likely to "bark" at you if you get in the way. As a high school kid and student of hers I took a few laps around the track for not minding my manners.

Having survived and healed, I managed to qualify for several mid-May "vacations" to Carol's ranch on The Mountain with groups of my high school friends, where we were privileged to enter the real life of Carol and her friend Bev Martin. We packed fenceposts and rolls of barbed wire, stretchers and sledges and fencing pliers and nails. And not only did we get to pack these items up some of the near-vertical slopes Carol politely calls "fence lines," but we also had to grab and use them. We learned to speak an eclectic terminology where a "Ubangee" is a used fence nail you bang back into shape and pound in again—not too tight so that the fence can give and take snow loads and head-on charges by wild elk.

We untangled and spliced and stretched wire. We crawled through thorn bushes and rock piles. Most amazing of all, we took turns swinging a twelve- or sixteen-pound sledgehammer— we could pick which one—at a flat spot the size of a silver dollar on the top of a cedar fencepost. Our object was driving it into the mountain far enough to support a fence. Carol held the posts and let us practice this dangerous art. She put incredible trust in us, just girls, to learn to swing the heavy sledge straight, to hit the post just right so we didn't wreck the top of it or her hands.

Nobody had ever trusted me to do a job like that, and it's been a gift of confidence and courage I've carried around since then.

We didn't just work, of course. We rode horses, the nice ones that wouldn't try to buck us off, and we bumped around in the back of one red pickup or another 'way up some logging road, occasionally ending up at forest so deep and dark that nothing but the white trillium flowers could live and bloom under it.

One day Carol and Bev took us on a "little hike," which I remember as about thirty miles but was probably only fifteen. We climbed through successive meadows and forests until we got to Gabe's Peak and Wilson Meadow, still full of snow on a sunny spring day. We all got to see a mountain lion loping across a draw below us. We got sunburned sledding on our jackets, lunched while gazing at the left half of Idaho, then replaced the weight of our lunches with splendid-looking quartz-veined rocks and hauled them all the way home. I think Carol let us sleep in until seven a.m. the following morning.

One of the lucky things about returning to Carol's ranch the next spring was that we "veterans" got to help scare the liver out of the rookie crew by using Carol's wolf howl tape played on her tape recorder. I'm not sure which girl holds the record for crossing Bear Creek the fastest in the middle of the night in her bare feet and PJs having abandoned "sleeping out under the stars."

Once Carol had all the girls inside the cabin, she would rush out and fire a shotgun a couple of times and then come in to tell her shivering, wide-eyed campers that they'd survived "a close one." The astounding thing is that she'd never admit it was a joke. If you were a victim of her horseplay, you didn't know if for sure until a year later when you got to help put on the trick for the next group.

Taped wolf howls evolved to Bigfoot attacks. You can read about this elaborate hoax orchestrated by Carol in the last chapter of this book.

The food on Bear Creek was plentiful and delicious, probably made even more tasty by the thirty-mile hikes and the high-altitude fencepost packing. Carol's generous passion for living included steaks, corn on the cob, popcorn in front of the fireplace late at night and, most special of all, ice cream.

Ice cream doesn't keep well in summer, even in the frigid waters of Squaw Creek, so one of the most appreciated gifts you can bring up to the mountain is a half gallon or two of any flavor. The ice cream must be devoured on the spot, of course—its icy sweetness blending with the smells of dust and pine pitch and cedar and creosote.

Loggers and salt truck drivers and Forest Service hands who dealt with Carol in the salt-packing years learned early on that their infractions against Carol's cowgirl punctuality and fierce trail etiquette could be mitigated with a half gallon of the Boise Valley's finest ice cream.

This book isn't just about what Carol and Bear Creek meant to a bunch of high school kids. This book is really about The Mountain and the nine years that Carol and Bev hauled salt and chased cows all around it for the Payette Valley Cattle Association.

It was an unusual job for a couple of women in the late twentieth century, a politically correct thing to notice, but when I ask Carol if she sees her life as unusual, she says, "It depends on whose life you compare it to." And then she tells me a story about Irma Robinette, who more than kept up with her husband, Slim. The story as told by Carol goes like this:

> Slim rode for the Association for thirty or forty years, before there was a Forest Service. And then Irma could get right on a horse and ride right with him. One time he led a horse in that had bucked him off behind where my cabin is now. Orville said, "Well, aren't you going to get on him and ride him again and not let him buffalo you?" He said, "Nah. I'll slip him over into Irma's string. She'll never know the difference."

Carol was quoting Irma but also speaking for herself. "I knew what I liked to do and what I enjoyed and what gave me satisfaction, and it wasn't being in the valley," she said.

Women can do what they have to do, what they want to do, and that's it for the "woman" issue.

Carol's strongest identification is with the mountain rancher as opposed to the valley kind, for it is the mountain rancher she regards as unusual and somewhat beleaguered between various misunderstandings about cows, grazing, and logging. As a trained biologist with a lifetime of experience on The Mountain, Carol speaks the language of the environmentalist even as she debunks some favorite environmentalist assertions about cows and trees or points out a mountainside of seedlings in straight rows on Association ground or a full pasture of bluegrass growing under trees where it isn't supposed to be.

She asserts that every good rancher is already an environmentalist. She explains in detail what she means, and she offers an awful lot of good advice on how ranchers, cowboys, government people, tourists, and loggers can get along with each other. Her advice sometimes involves ice cream.

Ridin' The Mountain should be seen as a parable for work well done, connected to and dependent on the land, which is all of us, even if we don't know it or think about it.

This book is also an adventure, not spread out over the face of the earth, but riding into the same landscape again and again, in every season and in every light.

Carol knows which days at which elevation which flower blooms and she'll tell you its name. Listening to her stories, I've often thought of what writer Dick Nelson said of his real and metaphorical Alaskan island in *The Island Within:*

> As time went by, I also realized that the particular place I'd chosen was less important than the fact that I'd chosen a place and focused my life around it. Although the island has taken on great significance for me, it's not more inherently beautiful or meaningful than any other place on earth. What makes a place special is the way it buries itself inside the heart, not whether it's flat or rugged, rich or austere, wet or arid, gentle or harsh, warm or cold, wild or tame. Every place, like every person, is elevated by the love and respect shown toward it, and by the way in which its bounty is received.

As you read this book, I believe you will find that *Ridin' The Mountain* is an affirmation of these sentiments.

CHAPTER 1

WHATEVER IT IS
WE DO UP HERE

MY PARTNER BEV MARTIN and I had been working cattle on The Mountain for five years in August 1982 when a reporter for the *Idaho Statesman*, the largest newspaper in the state, left a message with our neighbors Joy and Denny Weaver. He wanted a personal interest story. We didn't have a phone.

I said, "I'm not interested. I'm not even going to go out and call him back. I don't want any newspaper people around here cause they could do us a lot of damage, depending on how they wanted to cover it."

"Well," said Joy, "You better go call him." She had come seven miles to give me the message.

Reluctantly I went down the canyon and made the phone call. I talked to Larry Swisher, a young writer. He wanted to come up.

I said, "To start with, how did you know how to get this number?" The Weavers' phone number had no connection with us to anybody who would look in the phone book.

He laughed and said, "Well, Dave Bivens told me how to get a hold of you." Dave had been a cattle owner, and I had worked for him until he sold out his cattle and went into politics. Since Larry was a political writer as well as a reporter, he had gotten to know Dave quite well. Dave had told him, "You better look those girls up and find out how a good cattle outfit's run up there."

I mellowed. I knew Dave would not sic somebody on us who would hurt us. I let him explain what he wanted, and we set a date and time when he and his photographer, John Blackman, could be there. I told him they should bring a lunch and a jacket, some gloves and boots. We would furnish the horses, chaps and other equipment. Two days later they arrived as planned, and a look at our busy life began.

Larry was a stout and big-boned eastern Idaho native. John was a wiry kid newly from New York. We walked down the lane to the corral, Larry walking with me and John walking behind us with Bev.

Larry said, "One of the women in the office offered me her donut pillow if I needed it." He explained that the woman had just had a baby, was done with the donut pillow and had offered it to him. Larry asked her, "How come? Why am I going to need a pillow?' She just laughed an evil laugh and said, Well it'll be here when you get back.' I'm not going to need that," he said. "I've ridden!"

"How much have you ridden?" I asked him.

"Well, I used to ride my grandpa's old plowhorses a little."

I had a hard time keeping a straight face. I told him, "You better keep that pillow in mind."

We got the horses ready, and John was taking pictures like mad. I said, "You better save some film for up top, cause you're gonna have a lot of picture takin' to do up there."

"I brought a whole gunny sack full!" he said. But yep, he ran out of film later!

We got the chaps out. I asked, "You fellows want chaps?"

John, the Easterner, was eager to find out what the West was all about. "Oh yeah! I'll wear chaps!" he said.

Larry refused. "Nah, I don't want them."

I said, "You probably ought to wear 'em; they'll make you feel better." He was still not interested.

We loaded the horses in the truck and started up Third Fork until we saw cattle. I said, "Why don't you guys just stay here with the truck. We'll round these few head up and get 'em started and then Bev'll take the truck and go on down and meet me down below." I knew we were going to have a long ride after that and thought they should save up their energy.

No. They wanted to ride right then. If they would known what the day was going to hold, they would have stayed in the truck. I knew they could not round up cattle and that anything other than road-riding would be too dangerous for them since we were working in old clear cuts. These areas are full of half-buried cable/rotted out stumps which leave leg-breaking holes. To compound everything in an old clear cut, the underbrush is thick and tall. You cannot see most of these hazards and the reject logs are

2

half rotted out and will collapse under a horse. Any major runoff will form a steep-sided gully or ditch and probably be covered with brush, so you will fall in it. Most horses hated to work these areas. My Arab, Skipper and Bev's part Arab, Dutch, were our best clear-cut horses. They seemed to take it all on as a challenge and would still get cows out.

We unloaded their horses. John and Larry got on and took off on a fast run up the road. When they came back, I said, "Now, fellers, normally we don't do that, unless we're chasing something. If you lose a shoe off of that horse, you're gonna be afoot before the day's out."

Once Bev and I had rounded up a few cows, I told them, "You can't go with me now." They wanted to ride over the ridge with me, didn't know how far it was or how rough it could get. "I just don't take people into these clearcuts on horseback. It's too dangerous for you and the horse. Get your stuff in the truck, and I'll meet you and Bev at the bottom. I'll guarantee you all the ridin' today that you want."

They minded like gentlemen, loaded into the truck and went with Bev ahead of the cows I was driving. They had plenty of time to get the horses unloaded. They were so excited getting ready to ride again that they forgot to put their lunches in the saddlebags.

I drove the cattle down and picked up a few more on the way. When I got down on the southeast end of Pole Creek Flats near a swampy area, the cows peeled off and went to the swamp where there were other cows. Bev, John and Larry met me there by the swamp while I dug out thirty-five or more cows and one bull.

What a mess! It was a fierce area—timber, downed timber, wash outs and swampy. There was no sense in getting four horses stuck in that stuff, especially with two greenhorns, so they just watched.

After that the four of us drove the cattle up the dusty trail toward Green Field Flats. John was shooting pictures all along from his horse. We turned off the trail and up a draw. The goldenrod was in full bloom in there. Gorgeous. We had black Angus, black Ballys and Hereford cattle. The goldenrod up above their backs made a beautiful picture. Color you would not believe.

We got up top of the draw, then drove them down another logging road for a hundred yards, cut them up the next draw to the next road and up another draw. We finally dropped them way high on the mountain where we usually started packing salt.

Photo by John Blackmer, Idaho Statesman

**GOLDENROD. Cattle and cowgirls Carol and Bev head towards Green
Field Flats on top of The Mountain.**

I told the boys, "You better stop here, and we'll rest a little,
get a drink at Poison Creek." By now they had been riding an
hour or so. The water looked awful good. "This is Poison Creek,"
I told them. I took the tin can we had stashed there and dipped up
some water and offered it to them.

"What did you call this creek?"

"Poison Creek."

"Is it drinkable?"

"Well, I don't know," I said, drinking some. "Now, do you
want a drink?"

"Yeah, I'm pretty thirsty, but how about giardia?" Larry
said.

"I don't know. They haven't bothered me yet. Maybe they'll get to you, I don't know. If you want a drink, fine. We don't pack water with us in this country."

So they drank a little, and we got rested up, and then we rode even higher to Green Field Flats, and up to about eight thousand feet elevation. The lupines were in full bloom. If you did not like the smell of lupines, it could nauseate you. They were one mat of bloom in that area. The dogs got their picture taken rolling around in a snow bank next to lupines blooming.

Larry had a big notebook he would fill before the day was up, and John was taking pictures of everything. We told them why, how, where, when, what—answering about a million questions as we rode along.

After a while Larry said, "I'll never look at another cow and have the same feelings that I had before about open range and cattle on it and the rip-off the public thinks they're getting. You've really educated us today! I'll never forget this."

I thought, "Yeah, one of these days you're gonna end up in Washington D.C. writing stories, and maybe you can help the cowman out here. He needs all the help he can get." (And D.C. is where he is today, as this book is being printed.)

When we got to the top we showed them Cascade Reservoir far below with boats that looked like chips of wood and mountain range after mountain range stacked one on top of another into central Idaho. We could see the same thing up there, looking into Oregon at the Eagle Cap Wilderness area. Beautiful scenery.

We came across a fence that hadn't been put in right and needed to be fixed, so we stopped the tour to do that. We didn't have a sledge hammer to pound the steel posts, so I picked up a big rock and started pounding on that post with John clicking away on his camera. We must have looked like stone age cowboys. We took another break and shared our candy bars.

As we came down the canyon I said, "In a minute, fellas, I want you to slow down, and, John, you'll want a picture. Stick your right foot out a little in the stirrup, and aim your camera right down your leg. You'll get a fantastic picture."

When we got to the spot, I pulled my horse up with Larry behind me and John behind him. "I don't want a picture, I don't need a picture! Let's get out of here!" John yelled. Looking over the toe of my boot I could see the creek roaring fifty or seventy-five feet below.

After a while we came to where we would cross the creek, stopped, and divided up the last of the candy bars. John, the Easterner, said, "I know now why you wanted us to be in chaps."

Larry asked, "How come?"

"I'm not near as sore as I would have been without chaps."

Larry said, "Why didn't you tell me that's why you wore chaps? I can hardly wiggle!"

I laughed. "We tried to get you into 'em but you didn't want to. Take heart. you only got about five more miles to ride, all downhill in the rocks, and you got some beautiful scenery on the way, waterfalls and stairsteps dynamited out of the granite. It'll be a neat ride, so you won't notice your pain."

After about five hours of sitting in the saddle Larry was shifting in his saddle from one side to the other saying, "I might need that donut pillow before we get out of here!" He went on. "My boss told me this is an official assignment and that I'm covered with workman's comp." Larry said, "I looked at him and asked, 'What does that have to do with a horseback ride in the mountains? I'm going out to ride with a couple of women. It isn't going to be any big deal.' My boss just laughed and said, 'Young man, when you get done with that ride, I predict you're not going to be able to sit in a chair and type, and it's darn hard to lie on your belly and use a typewriter to write your story!' Now I'm beginning to realize what he was talking about."

We were still answering questions all the way back to the cabin in the truck, although they were not nearly as fast coming as during the day. And by the end of the trip those young men were bow-legged!

We invited them to stay for supper and assumed when we got to the corral that they would help us unload and unsaddle the horses. Instead, Larry said, "If you don't mind, I'm going to the house!"

I said, "Go ahead, stretch out on the bed out on the porch, or go in and lie on the davenport. It isn't locked." John started to help us feed, and then it hit him. He sat on a bale of hay until we finished.

By the time we got in the house to start fixing supper, it was seven o'clock. They had been with us ten hours and on their horses eight, not nearly as hard a day as we were used to.

While Bev and I made supper, Larry could not hold still. He went from one chair to the next, to the hard steps going upstairs, to the recliner, to the swivel rocker. Then he would walk. He would fidget and widget while he was eating, but he was so hungry, I guess, that he didn't have any trouble sitting at the table to eat!

I told them, "This is just like a field trip. I want to see you eat, I don't want to see you be picky. If you don't like it, that's something else, I don't care. But if you're hungry, eat it. That just suits me fine." What a feast we had, and they did eat.

I fried a huge skillet of fresh spuds and onions. Bev did her specialty of sourdough biscuits that we ate with cow butter and huckleberry jam. We had fresh steak, roasting ears and tomatoes. For dessert there were sliced peaches and cookies. And when we were done, there was not one spud left, not one crumb of anything. Those men ate until they could hardly get up off their seats.

Larry and John wrote us a letter later, thanked us for everything and said how much they appreciated their time. They did not need their worker's comp after all, but they sure knew they had been on a horse for awhile! John said, "I'd rode my grandpa's horses, plow horses, work horses type thing once in a while when I'd go out to the farm, but I'd never ridden any to speak of." He said this was the most challenging and difficult photography assignment he had handled because of the dust and being on horseback.

Two days later was my birthday, and Bev and I were sitting outside recuperating from our day's work when a couple of our friends drove up waving a newspaper out the window. "You made front page!" Sure enough. The Statesman put a color picture of us on top of the mountain with our dogs and wrote a story that covered almost half of the front page and another half page inside.

Our friend Denny Weaver and his truck-driving buddy Bob saw the article in the newsstand in a restaurant in Ontario, Oregon. Denny bought all the papers in the stand. The lady at the counter said, "What're you gonna do with all these?"

"These are my friends and neighbors," Denny said.

We ended up with coverage all over the Northwest. Some magazine from back east even put an article in. The story apparently made it into a national wire service because one of my former students heard it, a long ways out of this area, on the radio. And Jesse, one of our friends, had relatives in Louisiana, and she sent them the article from the Statesman. One of her relatives called her and said "Why, I've seen that on TV down here."

Jesse said, "You're kidding me."

She answered, "No, that very same picture was flashed on TV and they had a little feature on it one evening."

Chapter 2

HOW WE GOT HERE

RANCHERS OUT IN THE HIGH DESERT look up at our country at eight-thousand feet elevation and respectfully call the area "The Mountain."

The Mountain is part of the west mountain range in Gem County, Idaho, and has numerous subalpine meadows, large and small. These meadows are dotted with high-altitude trees and shrubs, fringed with flowers. The native grasses are quick to grow in the short growing season and make a dense mat in the meadows. Some meadow areas are swampy and lush.

From the home corrals to Green Field Flats, the largest meadow in the allotment, is about fifteen miles. The main peak, Snow Bank Mountain, has a radar dome and station manned year-round. Further south, West Mountain pokes a hole in the sky and sports a fire lookout, which is not always manned even in summer. To get there you ride a Government trail up "Jacob's Ladder" (a steep boulder-strewn trail) and eventually come out at "Hangman's Tree" close to the lookout.

In both of these peaks and in Miner's Flats are old mineral mines. You can see a lot of glacier scarring in the granite up there and in the upper reaches of Squaw Creek Canyon.

Our job on The Mountain has meant hard work, long days and many difficulties, but we have fond memories, and I would not trade my experiences for anything.

Through the years Bev and I have purchased more and more private land near our place until now we own almost sixteen hundred acres as well as twenty-five to thirty miles of fence. This has been an accumulation over many years.

I'll start at the beginning to tell you about our life here on the mountain and how we got here.

My father, Myron Shultz, bought 540 acres eighteen miles north of Ola, Idaho, in Gem County, in 1948. I was at a very impressionable age, loved to ride horses, be in the hills, and do things by myself. Dad was crippled up with arthritis in his hips, so during my college years I did a lot of fencing for him. I knew for a long time that I wanted to ranch but went through college and became a high school biology teacher.

I had taught school three weeks when my dad was killed in a truck accident. Mom and the ranch needed some help, and my sister Myrna was ready for college. My brother Wes was more mechanical and liked heavy machinery, and he lived a long ways away. I knew that running this place would not be an easy task, but I like challenges, so I took it on.

Bev Martin and I met when her Caldwell field hockey team competed against my Adrian, Oregon, team. For five years Bev came up to the ranch off and on and helped out. We also worked several years for Dave Bivens and the Payette Valley Cattle Association. The Association was a group of ranchers that put their cattle together on Forest Service land during the summer months and hired cowboys to watch over them.

When a job opened up on the mountain working cattle for Dave's association, we decided to apply. No other women had ever done this job before, so I'm sure they were a little nervous about us. But Dave knew we were capable and stuck his neck out for us.

We got the job. For nine summers Bev and I were riders for that association, from 1977 to 1985. Since we were both teaching school, we would drive the cattle in the summer and go back home in the fall. We didn't live in the Association's cow camp, but in better accommodations—my cabin that sits on Bear Creek. Later we came up on weekends through the fall. It worked out great.

Having two bosses could be a challenge, but we were lucky to have the best to work for, both from the Association and from the United States Forest Service. Dave wasn't the Association president, but he was our mentor. He was great, and we were happy to answer to him about anything to do with the cattle. He would come out about once a week, and I would pick his brain to find out how to do a good job. He taught us a lot.

Our Forest Service supervisor, Jack Colwell (who started when we did as the assistant range manager, right out of college), was in charge of the land itself, the fences, and the rules of the Forest Service for cattle on the range. Jack knew women could be capable at a job like this and told us he had no compunction at all about it. He would say, "My mother could out-work my dad and me both." They had a lot of confidence in us, and that made our job a whole lot easier.

When the Payette Valley Cattle Association began keep-ing books in 1917, there were over twenty ranchers in the group, all from the Payette area. They ran 2,100 pairs of cow/calf units. Their rider and his helpers would start out in the Washoe area near Payette, Idaho, on the Payette River in March and collect cattle from ranches all the way up to the early spring range of sagebrush country.

In June the cattle would be driven over the range of moun-tains into Squaw Creek. It would take several drives when they needed to travel so far, so the rider always had extra help for the trip.

In those days a rider got paid one dollar a head for however long he stayed out on the range. He also got a dollar for each slick calf he branded. When we started doing this in 1977, the Forest Service charged the ranchers anywhere from fifty cents to a dollar per head. Now the fee is $1.50 per head per month (known as an Animal Unit Month or AUM) and no freebies.

There are advantages and disadvantages to the rancher in sending his cattle to the allotment (the area of land assigned by the Forest Service to a group of cattle). When it started, the allotment included around thirty-five thousand acres and was later cut to about twenty-five thousand. A disadvantage is that some stock definitely gets lost on that much land.

The Forest Service called the cattle owners "permittees," because of the special permit they had to use the allotment for grazing their cattle. They were the ranchers. There were several names for us riders. Probably because we were women, the first year the permittees kept their eyes on us. After that they left us alone and pretty well let us run things the way we wanted to. They believed in us.

There were four main ranch families that we dealt with: the two Craig families, the Uhrigs, and the Bivens. They were the neatest fellows to work for.

J. D. Craig was about Bev's and my age. He had bought his the outfit from his dad, Earl Craig, who later rode as a cow-boy out here. Their place was out by Crane Creek. J. D.'s favorite trick was trying to dump off the cows and wanting to scram rather than help drive them over Squaw Creek out into Third Fork Pocket. He would say, "I have a cement truck coming. I have to get home." I usually take the bait the first time, but when he tried that line the second year, I told him I thought the cement truck probably could keep turning; it didn't need any help. He grinned, stayed with us and helped us move the cattle.

J.D.'s uncle Lavelle Craig had a ranch of his own, too. He and his wife Chloe lived by Crane Creek Reservoir in high desert country. He always had a grin on his face and a gung-ho attitude. "Well, that cow died. Her calf will take her place on the mountain two years from now. That's all right." Lavelle and Chloe loved to come up, visit and fish.

Glenn and Kenneth Uhrig were brothers who worked hard and had some good looking cows. Kenneth was on his last year as president of the Association when we started.

The rancher we knew the best by far was Dave Bivens. Dave worked with his brother Jim, and it was their father, Walker, who started this outfit before there was even a Forest Service in here.

A long time back when Bivens drove their cattle, they would start from their Payette ranch headquarters. In good weather it took them five days and sixty miles of rocks, sagebrush, pine trees, hills, and rattlesnakes and a bunch of permits to get to the allotment. Four to six cowboys worked about three hundred pair of cattle. At times they would have up to seven hundred pair with all the other outfits that joined them. In 1977 they started trucking them in to the Association's pasture ten miles from the allotment.

The chuckwagon on Bivens' early drives was a rubber-wheeled cart with canvas bows, pulled with a team of horses. They used that cart until the mid-1950s. One year they tried a regular chained-up pickup. It rained all the way in, and by the time they hit the "road" around Dodson Pass, just before dropping into Squaw Creek, it was a quagmire!

They hooked five saddle horses to that pickup with lariats to get it through. Two horses on the uphill side kept the pickup upright; three were up front pulling through the mud. Once they got on top, they put the front horses in the back to be the brakes while going down the pass. That might have been the last time the pickup was used for a chuck wagon.

Bivens eventually retired and sold out to a millionaire sheep man, Phil Solen. Five years later Solen sold out to the J. R. Simplot Company. Eventually Lavelle Craig sold out to Simplot also, so that in 1992 the permittees were just J. D.

Craig, the Uhrig brothers, and J. R. Simplot Land and Live-stock.

The Emmett Ranger District is one of the biggest in the Northwest and has eleven or twelve different grazing allotments on it, including a couple for sheep. Considering that our allotment was one of the smaller ones with only 26,000 acres on it, that is a *lot* of land for them to keep tabs on!

The Forest Service was good to work with; I have nothing but high praise for them. They were trying to do the job with their hands tied politically and financially. They tried to make our lives easier. Dick Estes and Jim Lancaster were the head rangers when we were riding. They were top-notch men, gentlemen from the word go. They knew their stuff.

Jack Colwell was our immediate Forest Service boss and for nine years a great source of information and directions when we needed it. Whenever I asked what I called a "dumb question," he never made fun of me, just gave an honest answer.

Here is an example of how much Jack believed in us: One day Jack saw a block of salt sitting right beside one of the roads up the mountain. We had put it there for the cattle we could not catch, the renegades. When Jack finally caught up with us, he asked, "What in the world are you doing with that block of salt?" (It wrecks the growth of grass and makes a real mess.)

"Calm your liver. We'll pick it up," we said, and told him why we put it there.

"You can salt anywhere you want if that's how you're doing it," he said.

Jack told us later that during the first year we were riding, the Association was in trouble—which explained why one or more U.S. Forest Service men came around at least four days a week! They were looking for evidence to justify cutting the Association's cow numbers. There never was a cut.

He told us, "You gals saved the Association's neck!" Over time we found out that our allotment started out not just in trouble, but judged to be the worst of the eleven they were supervising. After we had been there a while he told us, "This allotment is the best out of the eleven!"

After our first or second year, we never saw Jack. If I wanted to ask him a question, I had to come out seven miles to a telephone, call the office, and leave him a message. That worked for me, because I never have liked people looking over my shoulder; just get out of my way and let me do it.

He was like that. When it came time to put cattle higher on the mountain, I asked him about it. "Jack, I don't know whether I should put more up or not. What do you think?"

And he said, "I'm going to leave that entirely up to you two gals. You've been up there, you've run this association long enough, I've got one hundred percent faith in what you're doing." He left it at that.

Every year before the cattle were brought into the allotment, the Forest Service range management folks came in, and we all went on "the range ride." We toured the area, and they decided on the date they would let us turn the cattle in and how many, and generally go over the ground rules with the permittees and the riders. It was kind of a get-acquainted, howdy, how-are-you-again type thing every year. I always enjoyed it.

Since there are so many logging roads, the rides were done in pickups. When there was no snow blocking the way, they could drive to six thousand feet elevation and look up into the high country meadows.

Whatever they did to improve "our" land, we greatly appreciated it. Sometimes they would bring in high-content nitrogen fertilizer and put it on individual larkspur plants up at Pole Creek. (Larkspur is highly poisonous to cattle, and the nitrogen kills larkspur on the spot.) Another time they beautified the countryside a little by bringing in a Cat to do some work. Up at the unimproved campground somebody had abandoned an old hippie-type yellow van. The work crew stripped it, crunched it with their Cat, dug a hole, and buried it. Bev and I threw on some grass seed.

Record keeping was one of the most time-consuming parts of our job. This we did to make reports for our bosses. Bev kept daily journals. She carried a little notebook in her pocket and jotted down notes while we were out and about. When we would come in, exhausted from hard physical work all day, we still wrote the day's journal.

At the end of each month, I carefully typed up what we did that month and made reports at the end of each contract year, for the permittees and for our Forest Service bosses. The reports included the number of hours we spent salting, shoeing horses, driving cattle, the amount of time we spent on pack-horse work, cleaning trails, fixing spring holes, or out at night prowling.

We had a dead cow list: Who lost which cow and where. We would put in recommendations of what we would like to see done next year. For our own sakes, we recorded how many hours we put on each horse. This helped us keep them healthy and not overworked.

Just before we quit working for the Association, one of the permittees went to a meeting in eastern Oregon with people from the Forest Service and the Bureau of Land Management. He told us what happened. The Forest Service representative spoke to the group with one of our typed reports from the year before in his hand. He told them about the improvements we had made on this mountain. The people were dumbfounded. He said, "I about popped my buttons, too, because they were my girls, and my cattle, and my allotment."

The Association had eight sets of riders from 1917 forward. Here are notes about some of the riders I knew best.

Slim Robinette, their first cowboy, held the record for a career at the job at thirty-six years with only one year off. He was a small man, but he knew his cows and his work. When he started, there was no United States Forest Service, and regulations were almost nonexistent. Today you could write a chapter in an ecology book with all the rules. It was hard for even well-educated people like Bev and me to keep up with it all!

Slim was still riding when my father bought our ranch 1948. I remember visiting with him and his wife Irma. One fellow said he was the world's worst fence builder. If he couldn't do a task from a horse's back, he was not interested.

Slim was always trying out something new. His old saddle blanket rug was soring up too many horses in the hot weather, so he had an Emmett tire shop fix him four separate rubber inner tube squares with an air stem on each. He pumped these up, put the rubber next to his horse, saddled up and away he went. Going downhill his saddle would slip, and he would lean backward and let out a little air. He thought it was great until he realized the rubber had completely scalded the hide of his horse, and all the hair was coming out! He had to turn that horse out all summer with very peculiar saddle marks. The inventor threw his air sacks in the stove.

He never was satisfied with just catching a horse but had to go out and spend half the morning hunting up his remuda. He would run them into the pole corral and then rope them. He never was known to walk up to one and catch it.

Irma was quite a cowgirl. I was in high school when she told me one day, "Kid, don't you ever learn to shoe, then you won't have to do it. It is so blankety-blank hard!" She would not show or tell me anything else.

She must have known that sooner or later I was going to try. She did eventually teach me how to put the right side of the nail on the shoe and a few other tips I always remembered.

Another rider was Walt Young. Always a true gentleman, Walt was still riding into his seventies when he had lots of snow-white hair.

One day Walt told me about riding and visiting with a college student doing summer engineering work. The "young sprout," (as Walt referred to him) asked, "Aren't you getting too old to be riding that foxy horse all day long?"

Walt answered, "If the good Lord had intended for me to walk, he'd a made me with four legs," then took his horse down the side of the mountain.

Two old fellows, the Gill brothers, were living here when we bought the ranch. Years ago, Jim Gill rode the train to Idaho from Grand Junction, Colorado, looked the country over and liked it. His brother rode and rove out about thirty head of horses. Took him a month to ride from Grand Junction, Colorado, cross country to the Emmett area. There weren't many fences in those days.

Jim Gill packed the U.S. Geological Survey team into central Idaho for some of the original surveying done in there. He was also a bear hunter. By the time he got so he couldn't hunt bear any more in this area, he was pushing bear number three hundred that he had killed. They ate a lot of bear meat.

Jim was never known to overload his packhorses. One time he got on his saddlehorse with a backpack on his own back, and somebody asked him what in the world was he doing. "Well," he said, "I didn't want that old horse to have to pack so much, so I put 'er on my own back."

Those brothers wintered in our old rock house on the home ranch one winter, and winters could get fierce and long with six feet of snow. They somehow pulled in a long green log into the house. The house was twenty-four feet long and had a huge rock fireplace. As the winter wore on, they got cabin fever and stopped speaking to each other. The stove was on one side of the house, and the guy on the other side would cross over to cook, but except for that they each stayed on their own side of that green log and didn't talk to each other for the last part of the winter.

When our rider contract was over every fall, the Association would send in a rider for fall work and on into October. In the beginning we stayed long enough to break in the new guy. We would stay in our cabin, and they would stay below us in what we called "cow camp"

Chet Slater was the first fellow they sent in. He was young, with lots of ambition, and to this day I'm sure he's a very successful rancher. He had his own stock truck and horses. He had a friend, Big Mike, who came in and helped out occasionally.

The next year Big Mike took over. Bev had gone off to school, so I helped Mike. He was a character. He had a horse trailer, all kicked in every which way, but did it roll down the road! His saddle was in the same shape. He needed a dog, so I let him have Jiggs, a blue heeler.

Mike didn't have a mean bone in his body, and Jiggs really liked him. Mike's uncle, a wholesaler, looked out after him but didn't know what to send Mike in to eat, so he sent him a case of eggs. Thirty dozen eggs! And a great big ham. Mike's refrigeration wasn't exactly plentiful, so he came up one day, and said, "I don't know what I'm going to do with all that. My eggs are getting old, and the ham's beginning to mold."

I asked, "What are you feeding Jiggs?"

"Dog food."

I said, "Start feeding him eggs. He loves 'em. And he'll eat your ham, too."

One day I'd gotten busted up pretty good, so I took some pain pills and went to bed early that night. It had been raining, and I had watered the lawn, so it was pretty muddy.

The dogs just had a fit, barking and howling. Finally I got up and went into the main part of the cabin. I couldn't figure out what their problem was. There was a full moon, and a lot of shadows through the trees.

Eventually I took my sore body back to bed, and they started howling again. I got up and brought Jiggs in the house in case it was a two-legged predator, and left the other dogs outside. I figured Jigg would inhale an intruder and spit him out in little pieces. I sat up on the edge of the bed looking out the window. My rib cage was killing me.

Then I saw what looked like a bare human head and shoulders standing up. I thought, "Mike isn't that kind of a guy. He's just not the kind of guy to come up and visit at two o'clock in the morning. He's not crazy." Sometimes we would talk until midnight, but he wouldn't do this—would he?

I sat there and watched and wondered, "What do I do?" The dogs were still having a fit when, all of a sudden, the figure dropped out of sight and was gone. I thought, "Well, I bet it was a bear."

The next morning, there was a neat bear print in the lane. When I told Mike about it he said, "Huh! I might be dumb, but I ain't crazy. Do you think I would come up around your place at night? I don't need my head ventilated!"

The next fall the riders were Orville and Aloisia Harris. They had their own horses, their own pickup, stock truck and the works. All they lacked was the dogs, and of course we had the dogs! We told them we would furnish the wood, the stove, the propane, the house, the whole works. All they had to do was do the cowboying job—and most of that was pickup work—and keep the cattle off the creek.

Orville was not one to say, "Oh, that's a man's job, a woman can't do it," or the other way around. He had a lot of respect for women. He is a good cook in his own right, but not quite as good as Aloisia! Many a time we would be working, and by late Sunday night there would be a stack of dishes from the weekend. Orville would pitch in and do the dishes. He would just tell us to get on our way and get going, because we had a big two-hour drive to get home. "And get cleaned up so you'll get a little rest before you go to school the next day and face those kids."

One day he came in when Bev and I were eating supper. He said, "I'll do those dishes tonight, girls; you just go on." There weren't many dishes on the counter to wash.

I said, "Well, you better not. We better help you."

"Nope, I'll do 'em," he said. So I put the dishwater pan on the stove to heat up, and he started washing. Well, when he got done, I started dragging them out from under the sink, out of the oven, and out of the cupboard. He swore I dragged them out from under the bed, but I know that wasn't true! We'd had company, and we had a lot of dirty dishes! We washed for an hour.

We began to notice that beside the stove there would be a little stick three or four inches high which we would throw in the fireplace so we wouldn't trip on it. Next week we would come back, and there would be a stick again. Finally, after several times of that, we asked, "Hey, what's that stick for?"

Aloisia said, "I can't reach the light up there without standing on a stick, and every time you girls are here, I have to go hunt up a new one!" That stick stayed there for a good many years after that.

One of Orville's favorite sayings for when an old cow started chasing him was "She was a-blowin' snot down both my hip pockets."'

The other fall rider the last year or two was Doc Norris Hyde, the veterinarian. Doc was good with a horse, good with cattle, and a man who knew what he was doing. I don't think the permittees fully appreciated what Doc did for them. He was a quiet type of fellow. You never knew he was around half the time. He could be on his horse under a tree over there, and you would never see him. You would ride or walk right by him. But he could hunt bear and chase cows.

One day at the crack of dawn, Doc's dogs started baying at a bear right at our back door! Doc was yelling at them, and that bear and the hounds went the rounds. If he killed everything he had run, there would never be a bear left. He might kill one a year and he might kill none a year, but he had a lot of fun.

His dogs were Redbone hounds, and well trained. We took one of his dogs with us riding, and we actually got that dog to try to bark and not howl.

Our last year Ted Campbell came to be a fall cowboy. We took him riding up to the top of the mountain, to show him the area. He had a big horse used to the high desert and in good shape. I had my big Arab, and Bev was on Dutch, who is part Arab. On the way home we lost Ted for a bit, so we waited until he caught up. He was walking, and his horse was about half dead. The horse had had it! It took better than a week of babying that horse to get him back on his feet. Bev and hadn't gotten our horses off a walk all day long.

The year after we quit working for the Association, the regularly contracted summer rider quit long before permittees knew about it, so Butch McNair finished the year. Butch had a heart of gold and could handle a cow or a horse like nobody's business. He could put a good shoeing job on a horse. I really liked Butch.

Butch was never one for much fancy equipment. One day he stopped in when he was coming down the road. He was leading two packhorses, and his little girl, about eleven years old, was in the rear on Uhrig's buckskin horse.

The halters on his horses were old lariat pieces, tied up for a bosal and twine for a headstall. It was all sort of a halter and bosal tied into one with baling twine, and it was a big mess. Saddle blankets on the pack horses were really bad. One had remnants of a gunny sack, full of holes, for a blanket under the Decker packsaddle, and the other looked like a big blue egg carton with a large piece of orthopedic foam, rough side up, sticking out for about a foot or more all around, more than needed. Perched on top of it, like a skull cap, was a worn-out chunk of hair pad under a wooden crossbuck pack saddle. On it, he had the red trays for packing salt, tied on with baling twine and bright yellow poly rope. And the third cinch wrapped around all of it.

He said he could only pack three 50-pound sacks per horse, one on each side and one on the top. And then they all three would be on one side till he straightened them, and then the other side, or over on the horse's neck, or up between his ears. And he was really disgusted. I asked him if he had the black salt trays down there, and he nodded yes. He says, "I'm sure not going without it next time." I told him about the steel running "W"s to hook the trays to the Decker with. Yes, he had seen them, but he didn't know how to use them, or if they would even work.

UP TOP WHERE THE WIND ALWAYS BLOWS
Carol on Gigi, leading packhorse Ace, loaded with our "camp." We
had been cleaning and marking trail.

CHAPTER 3

OUR PLACE AND THE OUTFITS WE USED

OUR COW CAMP CONSISTED of the cabin on Bear Creek that I had bought from my father, several outbuildings and corrals. We call this place "The Upper Ranch," or the "Bear Creek Corrals," or just "the home ranch." The cabin itself had two rooms with a bathtub in the bedroom and a gas water heater back in a corner nook.

The place had no phone or electricity, so we cooked, heated our water, and kept things cold with propane. We used the nearest neighbor's phone seven miles away if we ever needed one.

Five big steps away from the cabin in slick rainy weather was a birch-lined two-seater "biffy." The outhouse. It had an eight-foot hole I had hand-dug years ago. There was a reason for the two seats: bald-faced hornets. They seemed to like to get down there where it's cool in the summer! We would kick the throne while stepping in, then take a willow stick, fish around in the hole, making sure both holes were open to give those hornets a sure way out of there. If we didn't do all that, more than likely we would get took. A bald-faced hornet can deliver a pretty good bang for the buck. That didn't happen very often!

We also had a bunkhouse and woodshed combination built twenty feet from the house. It was sixteen by thirty-six feet. A third of it was bunkhouse; two thirds of it woodshed. A large auxiliary woodshed was built in the early eighties to store the tractor or the ATV. Nearby we built the original rawhide

Bev Martin getting some water to boil in Miner's Flat. The steak came later when the fire had turned to coals.

shack, where I braided rawhide and Bev braided horsehair hat bands and other items. We used the bunkhouse for boys when I had biology field trips come out there.

We extended the ten-by-ten tack shed to make two rooms, leaving a wall in between with a wide door, so we could have extra hanging room. And we even had a corral biffy. We backhoe dug that hole, a little over seven feet deep into the rocks.

The machine shed was twenty-four by forty-eight feet, half of it fully enclosed. We built the whole works in 1988 with raw materials and the help of a few friends. Denny Weaver helped us with the backhoe on the difficult stuff, setting the heavy green uprights. Gloria Fastebend came one 4th of July and helped Bev put the steel roof on. Doc Olson helped us build two twelve-by-twelve doors that go on it and hung them on the sliding dollies.

There was also an old red Forest Service building beside the machine shed that we used for storing petroleum, paint and grass seed. Our 25-foot steel arching bridge over Bear Creek went from the house and wood shed complex over to the rawhide shack and down through the little pasture to the corrals.

Our handkerchief-sized lawn around the cabin kept the dirt down, made it cooler, and gave us a nice place to have a big barbecue when we had company. Our water system was gravity fed. We put it together in 1992. It had six thousand feet of pipe, dropped almost six hundred feet into the bottom of Squaw

Creek, and then came seventy-five feet the hill to the house. Sometimes it didn't work so well, but our spring was good.

Mr. Ewing homesteaded this piece years ago. He was a former state senator from the east. When he was diagnosed with tuberculosis, his doctor sent him West, telling him he had to get out of politics and the East if he was going to live.

Mr. Ewing took a bath in that creek every day of the year and went stark naked year around. He lived about three miles upstream from a school house, but his biffy was a big long heavy rope hung on a cottonwood limb out over the creek. He would make a run and grab that rope, swing out over the creek, do his thing and be done. Finally someone modified the rope so that the next time he swung out, he went into the creek.

Mr. Ewing's clapboard shack was still standing in the brushy creek bottom with a big lilac bush beside it when my father bought the place in 1948.

The upper ranch sat entirely within the Boise National Forest. It was all deeded property, and we were always thinking, "Maybe someday they will kick us off this place." So in the early 1980's, Bev and I bought my brother's place, which we called "The Lower Ranch." It was a quarter section and bordered on the National Forest.

Later we bought our winter headquarters on the old Steele ranch, nine-and-a-half miles from Bear Creek Corrals, and another nine-and-a-half miles into Ola from there. This place is now called the "lower ranch." It is out in the open. We could look out the two five-by-five windows in the living room to see a green meadow, creeks and some rimrock and pine trees. The road was plowed in the winter, and the mail came three days a week. We even had electricity!

There are two stories about how the line cabin in Green Field Flats was built. According to one story, Slim and another fellow cut the logs by hand and dragged them in with horses. By the time they got them up four feet high, they got tired of man-handling those large logs and put the roof over the four-foot walls. Then they dug out the floor to make it a taller cabin.

The other story goes like this: Slim and another old codger called One-Eyed John built it to full height. They had to saw the logs and dragged them in horseback, but laid no foundation of any sort. They packed in the roofing steel and the stove by horse from the camp, fifteen miles or so away. Then the heavy winter snows pushed the cabin down into the semi-swampy ground it was built on, until a year or two later the

Carol unloads Ginger on the truck ramp, ready to go to work.

men had to bring in big heavy railroad jacks on packhorses and jack it up and shore it up with new logs. They put in a set of log corrals and a pasture fence with old U.S. Forest Service telephone wire, which is extremely stiff, casually strung from tree to tree.

When we started this job in the spring of 1977 I had a 1974 four-wheeled drive Chevy—a three-quarter ton pickup with a custom-built horse rack that could hold two horses.

I could back into a bank, kick the horses out, and we would take out after a cow. The tailgate took a beating in the process. Once in a while it would get bent into a "V," and we would take off the tailgate, beat it back straight with a sledge hammer, put it back in, load the horses and go. Finally Joe Witty and the Adrian High School shop boys took it apart, opened it up with a cutting torch like a can of sardines and laid in two big steel pipes. That made it heavier than lead. I never had a horse that could wreck that tailgate!

The Chevy went a good many miles and hauled tons and tons of salt and a lot of horses, some of them kicking and tearing around. That pickup had seen some hard use before we started riding and looked like it had been through a wreck by the time we got done.

Those first two years we were living on a shoestring, so we used my family's old open two-cow steel stock trailer that my brother had made in college, years and years before. This trailer worked for horses that we didn't want to haul in a closed trailer, but dirt would get on them, and it was old and not trustworthy. One night we were pulling that trailer behind another pickup, when we saw something flash by.

Bev said, "I think that was a tire." The old trailer started bumping along, so we pulled over and, sure enough, the bearings had gone haywire. At least there wasn't a horse in the trailer!

We couldn't find the tire until the next day when we found it in a wet spot right next to the high raging water of Squaw Creek where it landed after jumping the four-wire fence out into a meadow. If it had gone in the water, I never would have found it! That incident helped me decide to buy something else.

Since my pickup was still working pretty good, we bought a new W.W. horse trailer. One of Bev's relatives bought two trailers in Oklahoma and piggy-backed them together; one was for us. We used it for the year. It was a beautiful bright cherry red, a nice outfit, but its tongue was too short, and it was too hard to back around in cramped quarters.

In 1978 we got a 1979 one-ton Chevy truck laid out for us special order as heavy as they could get it. We just ordered the chassis and cab, and when it arrived, Joe Witty at A.H.S. had his high school ag shop build a flatbed trailer and stock rack. We got innovative with the truck's tailgate by putting a spring from a garage door on it to help offload the horses. One fellow looked at it and said, "Shultz'll never load a horse on that thing. He can't get up it. If he gets on it and comes down, he'll slide clear back to Adrian!" We just smiled and went on building our thing. It has worked so well I've already gone through a couple of boards with it. Once a horse learned to walk it, that was the only way.

With that truck we could drive high up the canyon looking for cows, unload the horse and find the cattle before they knew we were anywhere around. It got to be quite a landmark, too. One year when the logging was thick and heavy, we put a CB (citizen's band radio) in it, and the loggers called us "the little red cowboy truck." They were good about keeping track of us on the treacherous roads. They would call down the canyon, "Little red cowboy truck, we are on pullout number 6, where are you?"

I might say, "I'm between pullouts."

Then he would say, "You better find a J-hook and get in it, cause I'm on my way—loaded." I was going up through those steep switchbacks and considerably smaller than his rig, so I would find a place to pull over and wait. They got a big kick out of watching us two gals work.

We also had a two-wheel drive Datsun pickup. I treated it like a four-wheel, and it went like a four-wheel drive. After about eighty thousand miles, its electrical system went belly up. But boy, it had been a hard eighty thousand. That Datsun was built well.

In 1985 I bought an S-10 four-by-four. At first I didn't like it. The first time I stepped on the wheel-wells with my boot, I left a permanent print on that flaky tin area. When we wanted to haul our Yamaha ATV four-by-four in it, we discovered my mashed-out wheel wells were in the way! With a sledge hammer I worked those wheel wells back up like I was kneading a loaf of bread. Then I drove the ATV in. That little pickup hauled a lot of salt and did a lot of good work.

I have a rubber-tired horse-drawn wagon, also built by my friend Joe Witty and his high school ag shop class. It has the seat up high on it. He broke a horse of his and one of mine to drive together, and used it to feed several hundred head of cattle in the winter. One day Joe hauled trusses for my new addition to the rawhide shack from the valley and brought my wagon on the load. We put the wagon tongue in, hooked up the horses, and we all went for a ride.

After Bev and I had been working for several years we bought an old, reconditioned Fergerson tractor. The guy who sold it to me helped me figure out what I wanted, how to rig the hooks on the bucket and welded them on for me. I told him, "You fix that just like it was going to your wife and she was out there working without you." We still use that tractor to clean corrals, load wood into the truck or pickup, tear up hillside pastures, rip and disk them to put in new seed.

We built two loading docks and a chute built on the edge of the road opposite each other and offset so that we could back right up and hit it on the level. We had to hurry getting the stock in the truck and trailer before a logging truck came, because we were blocking the road. One day I was in the corral and Bev had just loaded a horse when she heard a truck coming. She made a dash for the pickup. The trucker was coming around the corner too fast to stop, and my heart was in my mouth. I knew Bev had lost the race. But in a cloud of dust, between her and the truck, she made it.

In 1979 the Arabs brought us the gas shortage. We managed to get a half barrel here and there from begrudging station attendants. The shortage didn't slow down our work; we still put a lot of miles on because people were looking for meat since cattle prices were high. We would take the pickup and prowl at any time of night or day.

Two things helped us with the problems caused by the situation. One was CB radios in the vehicles, and the other was magnetic sheriff's signs. The signs helped us because people thought they knew who we were (even if we weren't), and what to expect from us. I think that helped cut our cattle losses. Whatever rig we were in, even somebody else's pickup, we always tried to get our Gem County Sheriff's Livestock Patrol signs on.

Our horses were an important part of our work force, which is a chapter in itself. Using them took a lot of equipment, and we didn't have it all the first year. I'm talking about a full set of shoeing tools and several boxes of horseshoes of different sizes, chaps, bridles and bits, reins, rommels, cinches, saddles, saddle blankets, quirts and whips. We had corrals, hay, and grain to keep in good shape. In this country, we couldn't get by without a roof over the hay in the wet winter months, so we built a hay shed twenty by thirty-six feet.

CHAPTER 4

SALTING THE CATTLE

RANGE CATTLE AND WILDLIFE, just like us, need salt, and one of our jobs was to make sure they got it. We set up areas on the range we called "salt grounds" where the cattle could come and lick salt. Each salt ground had a name, sometimes one that was given to them by the Forest Service and other times by the folks who set them up.

Our friend Gail was riding a green horse with us and got bucked off where we were going to put that salt tub. To this day we call it "Gail's Landing." "Dot and Dash" at Green Field Flats got the name because one day the cattle tramped down grass so that it looked like the dot and dash of a Forest Service trail marking. We called the north end of Green Field the "North Thumb," because it was up high on a big rocky thumb that stuck out.

We used the salt grounds set up by the old-timers as much as possible, and we had a lot of new ones we put in to help move the cattle off the creeks and away from the water. We used pasture that hadn't been grazed for years out on some of those big open high points.

We salted approximately forty salt grounds on each side of the allotment each summer. Each salt ground would have two, sometimes three tubs that held a hundred pounds of salt each.

When we packed the salt to the range, we tried to salt a few days ahead of moving the cows so that they were more likely to stay put.

The salt containers we used to hold the loose salt were rubber car and pickup tires turned wrong side out. We poured the salt in the "tub;" the cattle could get in it but couldn't break it. We called them salt tubs.

Tires were the best, but there were a few problems. Porcupines would sometimes chew on them. We would find tubs butted out of their spots by bulls, deer and elk. People would mess with them, too, and we would find them all tangled up in a brush pile or tipped upside down over kindling, Sometimes campers would take them. I saw a salt tub going out on top of some wood! I couldn't catch up with it.

To turn the tire inside out, we would cut the bead off one side, then put a knee in them. Grunting and groaning and saying things, we turned them. It wasn't easy. At first we didn't know how to do it. One day a friend came up to look at a sick cow on the ranch, and I said, "Hey, show me how to cut these tires." It was a hot day, and he told us that was what it took so the rubber would be a little softer.

He got his jackknife out and started cutting the tire. "It's hard work," he gasped. He didn't bother to pull away the bead he was cutting, and it was binding. Bev reached over and pulled the bead away, and cutting it was like running a hot knife through butter. Seemed like we were learning together.

The best tires for salt were retread factory rejects. They were ground down, ready to retread, not too heavy, and could hold a hundred pounds of salt easily. We would turn a tire, cut a plywood bottom and nail it to the bottom of the tire. One of our friends got a high school shop class to cut tub bottoms. They were cut perfectly round, fit beautifully, and had a hole drilled for the water to escape. But those things could be as elusive as a silver dollar on edge on a piece of glass! They would just roll down the mountain when they got empty. I said, "Baloney with this." I took the chainsaw and started butchering up half-inch plywood in oblong, nasty sizes so they didn't roll so easy. That helped. Some of our salt tubs have lasted many years.

The Forest Service books tell you the tubs need to be moved every year. That gets to be a laugh, because pretty soon you've got salt grounds all over the mountain and no grass. We convinced our Forest Service boss that except for the ones placed on the edge of trails and roads, we would leave them in one place and keep the mess in one spot.

Up in Green Field Flats we took one that had been put right beside the main government trail and put it back out where I remembered it as a kid. The cattle went back out there a half mile and kept the mess off the trail. We took grass seed back up and threw it in the dust where the tub had been, and got some grass to grow.

Our first year we had to drive seventy-five miles to Nampa, Idaho, to buy salt in paper sacks. We hoped it wouldn't get wet coming up country and throw it in the salt shed as soon as we got to the ranch. To pack it out on horseback, we would have to pour it into plastic sacks. We worked two tons of salt this way. I got so tired of resacking and breathing salt dust that I tried packing it in the original paper sack. I would roll it around and tie it with twine and stick it on my packsaddle. It made kind of a bulky load, and a time or two we ripped a sack, but a little gum or tape would fix it right quick, and we would get there with it.

On one of my trips for salt, I was standing in line. I had been riding in the brush, and I was scratched all over. You couldn't lay a dime anywhere on my arms or face without hitting a big old scratch. I was just standing there waiting, spinning my wheels and getting mad because there was no need of me having to pick salt up when it used to be delivered. And old cowboy and his wife were standing in the next line spinning their wheels, too. I had never seen them before. She looked over at me and said, "You must be from the Ola country."

I laughed and said, "Yeah, how come?"

She answered, "Because you've been riding in thorn brush."

Well, come to find out, he was Simplot's manager on Second Fork, and we became friends.

After the second trip down there for salt, I said to them, "Don't you guys deliver salt?"

And he said, "Oh, yes."

I asked, "How much is it gonna be?"

And he said, "Well, probably we could deliver it for nothing since you guys are buying quite a lot."

So I said, "Fine. Let's have some brought up."

The delivery service was pretty good except for a year or two when they had problems and no way to get a hold of us. Even when the salt was delivered, it would still kill a chunk of a day because we had to be there to unlock the gates and the building to put the salt in and sign the ticket. One year they were to have the salt in on Wednesday, June 1. We waited and fiddled around, worked around, and fixed fence and did this and that. Nobody showed up. I was fuming. We drove seven miles down to a neighbors to call. They gave me a story about how they were broke down and all this. I told him he better have a half gallon of chocolate ice cream with him, and if he didn't show in the morning, I would slit his throat when he finally did show, because I had too much to do to wait on a bunch of men!

Tom, a teenager who was visiting us, wanted me to braid him some rawhide, so the next day I said, "You scrape it, and I'll braid it."

We worked and waited for the truck to come. When nobody showed, we went down to the cow camp again and sat there and scraped, but nobody showed up. I was getting madder and madder. I came back up to Bear Creek for some stuff. When I got back the truck had pulled in, and Tom and the driver were unloading it. The kid in the truck kept eyeballing me with a worried look on his face.

As I approached, the driver blurted out something about ice cream melting in the front seat. I told him to keep on unloading, and I would go back and get some dishes, and we would eat ice cream right there. The kid said, "Oh, no. Never mind. That's for you!"

I said, "That's all right. Two half gallons is a little more than Tom and I are gonna eat at one sitting." He was a decent sort of fellow; it was the company that was giving us fits. I told him if I would have had anything to say about it, we would get our $1,130 worth of salt elsewhere, as their service was so bad. He agreed a hundred percent.

We sat there and ate and jawed a little. He said the directions from the Nampa office were to go above the U.S. Forest Service buildings and dump it. Then the boss told him "Be sure and take those gals some chocolate ice cream."

He said, "I thought my boss was bonkers until he told me how mad you were."

We killed a half gallon on the spot and ate the other one that evening. When you're out working like that and it's hot and dry and dirty, and you don't get ice cream very often, it doesn't last very long.

Another time they fouled us up down there on salt, and I happened to be in town. I dropped in on the company and he made some excuses. I said, "If you don't—"

"—I'll send a six-pack of beer with the guy," he interrupted me.

"I don't want any bottle. I want ice cream on that load, and if you don't bring me some, you'll be in for it." And, by George, the driver brought up chocolate ice cream.

"I couldn't believe my ears when he told me what I was supposed to bring," the driver said. "The company just doesn't do that!"

I told him, "The company doesn't stand up Carol very often, or you would be bringing me ice cream all the time."

Even in our first year I already knew where a lot of the salt grounds were, but after a lot of logging in the previous five years, there were lots of half-mile spur roads here and there and landings. We went up these roads in the pickup with salt and salt tubs, trying to figure out if we wanted a salt tub in a certain place or to see if there was an old one there already. It took hours and hours and gas galore to do this. We would get back at eleven o'clock at night, and then get up early the next morning to pack salt in by horseback or run cows back in.

Usually we would haul the salt to the grounds by pickup as far as we could go, and then go by horseback. One year I took salt on my "Japanese quarter-horse," a Honda 90 motorcycle. I could put up to a hundred pounds on the back of it! It would go around trees I couldn't get around with the pickup and was faster than a horse. Another time we used a team of horses and a wagon.

One year the Forest Service gave us a key to the Buck Mountain gate and told us we could use it to salt. If he knew it had been ditched, he didn't bother to tell us. I had an awful time getting in there. We had about a half of ton of salt in the back of the pickup and there were ditches every thirty-five to a hundred feet, depending on how steep the grade was. We just kept going, finally got it done, but I said some things.

Too often we could get into trouble with trees in the road, so we always had the saws in the pickup if we were salting or just out looking to see where the cows were or where we wanted to take them. More often than not, we would come home with a partial pickup load of wood because we had to cut it out of the way to get to where we wanted to go. That helped the camp wood supply, too and helped us clean the area so we could get back in later.

A horse could carry two hundred and sometimes two hundred and fifty pounds of salt, and we would take several horses. Even with horses, we would haul a chain saw with us. If we needed to, we would tie the horses up, fire the saw up and hope we didn't need more than one tank of gas. We didn't want to pack a can of gas on top of that salt if we could help it! Many times the chainsaw came in handy.

To salt the top of the mountain in Green Field Flats, we took salt in the pickup and headed up towards Pole Creek. We would go off onto some back logging roads in four-wheel drive and eventually end up at the "salt depot." We would leave about fifteen hundred pounds to a ton of salt, covered with plastic tarp and then come back the next day with our horses.

We would dump the extra fifty pounds a mile up the mountain so we would have loads later—ready to haul out on the flanks of the mountain. Some days we took a shorter run, the next day a longer one and so on. It was easier on the horses that way. The higher the elevation the less we loaded them down. We found a nice spot at the Poison Creek area, where we put the cantaloupe, the boiled eggs, and the peaches and things in the creek and ate them for lunch as we came and went.

We were packing the salt for our cattle, of course, but probably five or six hundred pounds of salt would be eaten by deer, elk and other critters! It was amazing to see how much the wild animals would eat when the cattle were gone. One day we accidentally dropped a sack on a big rock. Two days later we went back to discover a bear had gotten into the salt. There were claw marks and bear spoor around. He must have had a heyday. I wish I could have seen him.

One time we were packing an extra salt tub off the Third Fork Ridge. While coming down the ridge, somehow that tire got loose on Ace's pack. Bev was leading him on Rosie. Ace was kind of rough riding downhill, and it got shook loose.

The salt tubs (two tires nested inside each other, looked like one tire), rolled off the saddle and under Ace, rolled between Rosie's legs and on down the hill. Rosie's pretty steady, but she got her blood pressure up on that one!

Bev hollered just in time for me to look up and see those two wild tires coming. We almost had a first class rodeo up there, but we got out of the way, and they went zipping by us and hit a big rock. The tires split (unnested) and went on rolling their separate ways.

What a sight.

CHAPTER 5

CATS, BANTY ROOSTERS AND COW MANURE

PEOPLE OFTEN WANTED TO SEND CATS up to the Upper Ranch with us. I don't know why. I would tell them, "They probably won't come home." I knew that the great horned owls, the coyotes and snakes would eat them.

When were done at the ranch one year there was one cat we wanted to take home with us: Dogtail. He was tame only to your fingertip, but you couldn't catch him. Then I found him in a number zero packrat jaw trap. Luckily, a pack rat had pushed a gunny sack into the trap, and the cat got in the sack and didn't have even any abrasions on his leg. He went home in good shape only to get into a muskrat trap there in a ditch down in the valley and had to be put down.

Another time we hauled two cats in, and then the owner wanted them back. We put them in a telescoping orange box type thing and didn't think about tying the lid shut because it was a tight fit. We got as far as the cattle guard between the guard station and the cow camp. The cats were snarling mad anyway, and the noise of the cattle guard finished it off for them. The box flew off, and the cats vanished.We finally caught one of them, but the other one we never saw again.

We have also had cats come into the camp from campers who lost their pets. One was a beautiful Persian cat. He would sit and look at you and would eat if you would leave food, but you never could get your hand on him. I suppose something ate him, too.

Butch had an old black bobtailed cat that spent as much time up at our house as he did down at the cow camp a mile away. Butch was getting ready to move out, and as we drove in one Sunday evening, he had his gun out. We said, "What're you shooting?" and he answered, "Oh, killing the cats, 'cause I can't catch 'em and you can't leave 'em in here."

I told him, "Leave that black one. He'll be back up at the house, and we'll take care of him." We took him home, and he made a pretty nice cat for a year or two at Bev's place.

One of the neighbor ladies down the line a few miles gave me four roosters that looked half banty, but about three times as big. I turned them loose. They would fly up ahead of vehicles driving by on the road. One summer the logging trucks coming through there were really pushing it, wouldn't stop or slow down for anything. When Boise Cascade's woods boss stopped in, a man I knew very well, I told him that he needed to slow his men down, cause someday there was going to be a thousand dollar horse or my pickup or one of my mules jumping the fence, and they weren't going to be able to stop!

He said, "Aw, just throw a fence post in front of a truck when they come."

About then, one of those fancy little roosters came flying out, and I said, "See that thing? He's a fighting cock, and I'm raisin' 'em for a guy, and they're worth hundreds and hundreds of dollars, because they're purebred stuff. They are for breeding sock."

I was just feeding him a line of bull, and Elmer knew it, but he just laughed and said, "I'll tell them that."

I went on. "It won't be just chicken dinner! It'll be chicken all over you-know-what when they kill one of those things, cause they're worth megabucks, more than those good horses, even."

Later I was laughing and telling the neighbor about it, and she said, "You didn't tell him all that big a lie. They are, literally, half fighting cocks."

The logging trucks did slow down and started to come through there like civilized human beings. Elmer's philosophy was, "I don't care how big the truck or how big the machine, they ought to drive so they can stop on a dime. And if they can't, they're going too fast." I don't care who was logging, if he thought they were going too fast, he would slow them down. We appreciated that.

Bev and I are allergic to bees and hornets, so we pack bee kits with adrenaline. My first year I rode with an old saddle and a pair of saddle bags that I had hand-tooled and made while I was in college, and I kept my bee kit in that.

I got off to undo a pack horse with salt, up at a salt grounds. I got the nails out of the saddlebag to put a new bottom in the tub and noticed something sticking out of this side of my saddlebag. I gingerly reached down there. My bee kit had come open, and the hypo full of adrenaline had had a pretty tough ride. The needle had come out through the outside of the saddle bags and was bent at right angles when I took it out. I looked at that and thought, "I hope I don't have to use this. I don't know if adrenaline goes at right angles or not."

I still had my greasy riding gloves on. I carefully took that needle and bent it more or less back to normal. It was a little "S" curve, but it wasn't bad, and put it back in the kit. Years later Jessie Goodwin reminded me of a right-angled bee kit needle she had seen in the house one day. I guess I had a couple of them.

I remember going back and telling the nurse in my doctor's office that I needed another prescription for one of those kits, and she said, "You just got one."

I told her what had happened, and she was aghast. She didn't think it would work.

I said, "I know it'll work, I tried it. And it comes out of there kind of interesting."

She insisted that I buy another one. We needed a couple anyway. We kept them in the truck, in the pickup, and in the saddlebags. That way we always had one at the house, and the pickup, and always one when we were horseback.

One thing I enjoyed in the biological area was collecting plants for Dr. Pat Packard of the College of Idaho (now Albertson College) in Caldwell. For this I went to Green Field Flats and other places I wouldn't cover in my May biology field trip. Besides collecting for Dr. Packard, I was collecting for my own collection and for Adrian High School's botany collection of pressed plants. Dr. Packard said this was a wonderful area to collect because little botany work had been done there. Lots of collections had been made on the McCall side of me, on the east and on the west in the Cuddy Mountain and Weiser area but none right here. I took her dozens and dozens of flowers.

For two years I always took a plant press on the salt horse. Tuffy was the one that usually packed it. I've got pictures of that plant press with plants sticking out everywhere. They weren't the best done, because when you got done packing salt, you would put in about fourteen or fifteen hours that day, and they were wilted in the plant press and should have been opened up and redone. Sometimes I got it done, but a lot of times I didn't. But she always seemed tickled to get them.

The flowers were unbelievable. Since I am a biologist and have done quite a little flower identification through the years, it was very interesting to me to be able to ride in flowers all summer long.

On August 5, 1980, Jessie Goodwin and I were at Greenfield Flats. Bev was out to a conference. The flowers were so beautiful that you could not have painted them and said it was real. I ran out of film. Everywhere you look ed, it was like a rock garden There's no way to explain it. The brush bloomed as we would go up. The mushrooms would be working if it was a wet year, and we would pick mushrooms all the way to the top and bring them back in salt sacks. Being more or less a scientific cowboy, I was able to watch the flowers, listen to the birds and identify them. Bev learned a lot about the birds and flowers in the area just listening to me.

We spent a lot of time cleaning up after tourists, permittees, permittees' kids, whatever—down at the cow camp, in the camp grounds, wherever. We tried to keep things spiffed up a little. Down at the cow camp they had had some cat work done so they could get semis into the loading chute, and when you disturb the soil in this area you get mullein and bull thistle and sometimes Canadian thistle. If you cut it for two years and don't let it go to seed, then you can pretty well get a handle on it again.

We went down and cut thistle and mullein. We weren't asked to do this. We just went down and did it because we wanted it to look better and not look like a weed patch.

Another time we painted corrals and fixed things up down there. I painted the corrals up at the house, of course, and we kept our own corrals spiffy with good swinging, heavy steel gates, custom made at the Adrian High School shop. We painted the house, the gate and poles, and the truck with its steel bed custom-made at Adrian High school, and, of course, my propane tank.

It had to all be kept up or pretty quick it got down so far that it took more than paint. Then you would have to sand blast or simply start over. To us that was all part of the job. We kept both my camp and the cow camp spiffy.

Bev and I brainstormed about getting rid of the inch-wide, long leather straps with a heavy buckle that the Association had used for a hundred years, more or less, on their Decker pack saddles to hold the salt trays that they had also used for a hundred years. That was all right, but we packed a lot more salt than anybody else, and we wore out a lot of those straps. They would stretch out.

Junior Wholesale Saddle kept us in straps at a good price, but after a while, they all stack up for money. Besides that, things that stretch and let the tray ride wrong got to be a hassle. Bev and I would discuss the problem coming home with pack horses and wonder how we could do away with those darned old straps.

We got an idea or two, and one day we went down to Weavers.' I told Denny, "Get your thinking cap on. Here's what I want."

I drew him out what I thought would work, and he put another bend in it and said, "This'll work even better."

We came up with what we called "the running Ws"—a piece of steel bent into a three-dimensional "W." The bottom of the "W" fit around the half circle on the Decker, and the legs of the "W" stuck up and held the tray on. With those gadgets, we could put the Decker pack saddles on the pack horse and not have to put them up in front of the overhang for the dogs to chew on. We could throw the trays up there also.

That saved time when we were up trying to pack at places where it was hard to saddle. We used those "running Ws" the rest of the time. We always took an extra strap or two with us, just in case one broke.

The next year I had some heavier "W"s made at the Adrian High School shop. When I quit I left a pair in the salt shed for the Association. We kept two pair in our own salt shed. (I had paid for all of them.) They are really an innovation if you have something like pack trays to put it on and a Decker pack saddle. It just makes it work one hundred per cent of the time.

If you did not want to tie those trays down with your third cinch or a rope or something, you could do what worked for us.

We tied them to the back or front cinch to keep them from flopping while coming down hill on a pack horse. They're easily unhooked when you're ready to unload.

The cowboy who took over after we left came up one day with a "running W" in his hand and said, "What in the world is this? And what is it for?"

I told him what it was for, how to use it, and added our advice to be sure to tie it down. Well, he didn't tie it down and had a first-class wreck up on top of the mountain. He had salt and horses and mules and equipment scattered everywhere. He aborted his salting day and come home with his wreck.

But they really work if you use them right. I probably should get a patent on them.

One night we had some lightning and heavy rain. The garden was soaking wet because I had watered it before the storm.

Buck, my 1600-pound horse with a big hoof and a shoe that took a No. 2, and Dutch both got out of the corral somehow, and got out in that garden. There were holes the size of post holes punched in the spud row, in the corn row, in the spinach row. The spinach was eaten off, the corn was eaten off, and the spuds were knocked down. I didn't have much of a garden the rest of the year. They even ate my radishes.

Bev and were I chatting the other day while running some cows here on the ranch. Some of the things we talked about we felt we should go ahead and tell. Other things we thought maybe we shouldn't, but I said, "Nah, it's OK. We're never ridin' for those guys again."

We had one trick up our sleeves that really makes a difference on how the Association looks to John Blow tourist, to the environmentalist, and even to the range manager when he comes by.

We've got maybe two hundred miles of logging roads on this allotment. Some of them are blocked off. You can't drive on them. But still they're there. Hunters use them with their bikes, and they walk on them. And they're very noticeable. Cows use them. And if the cows are bedding on them, they're a mess with cow manure. And just plain walking across it—they'll leave a big cow pie.

I told Bev the first year, "That manure is really noticeable. We're going to do something about that."

"What do you have up your sleeve?"

"Watch this." I ran my big three-quarter Chevy over that cow pie and splattered it. Came back the next day—it had been hot—and, sure enough, there wasn't any cow pie around. After that it got to be a game, how many cow pies we could hit at ten miles or thirty miles an hour, and how far we could splatter them. When you would hit a bedding area on the road, if there was one, you had to back up and hit several of them.

When I got my truck with dual wheels, that got to be even more fun. You could really splatter the cow manure. It made a big difference. The permittees, the range management, the tourists, the ecologists, never knew there had been how many cows of what kind or when they had been there. We drove those roads every day after riding—looking for cows, seeing if they were where they weren't supposed to be, putting out salt or just plain "crap smashing," as we called it. It really worked.

We never did tell anybody, even the fall help, about it. The cows had come off early because of snow. One day Orville Harris said, "Boy, you know, there's getting to be a lot of manure on that road, and it's just hard to miss.

"Well, why don't you hit it?"

"Oh, I wouldn't want to do that."

I just laughed. We didn't say anything. We called it "recapping our tires." Makes the tires go farther when they're full of green manure.

It was even more fun when I got heavy lugged tires on that truck. The lugs are one inch wide. The whole distance between each lug is one inch, and you can dig a grave with those tires if you spin them.

When you get to hitting fresh cow pies and you turn that wheel just a little, it gets interesting. With your windows rolled down, you can hear that green cow manure go ffssshhttt! like that. It'll squirt clear across the road and hit somebody's car, a fisherman, or whatever.

It got to be quite a game to see how often and how far you could throw that stuff. If I were to ride again, that's one trick I would definitely do.

Hitting the cow pies tells you when and how many cows you had there. That was one trick of the trade I would reccommend to anybody.

It didn't hurt when they had a fall range ride one year and the county came in and graded the road. Any stray cow pies that might have escaped us got graded up and that looked great. That happened only once just before a range ride in the fall, and it was pretty nifty.

We burned a lot of wood and had a big wood shed. Finally I bought a woodsplitter that we ran by taking the wheel off the pickup and hooking the splitter to the hub. I had a little Datsun two-wheel drive pickup, and we would jack that thing up and split wood. Some of those logs would be three, three and a half foot across. You would just roll it over there and let the splitter take a bite. I never did have a piece of wood it couldn't split. We split a good many cords with that thing that way.

In August 1982 we had some hippie drug growers move in on Buck Mountain, and there was no key that fit the gate up there. The Forest Service staff working up there hit me up for a key because they thought I had one.

Pretty soon we got a new key and found out that these guys were up there growing marijuana. They were supposedly mining. One fall evening they came down and visited with us. They just wanted to see what we were going to be doing the next day or the next week.

One guy said, "We are going to pull a trailer house up there yet this fall, and we're going to winter up there."

You're talking about seven thousand feet, on a good winter six feet of snow with a trailer house, no water, no facilities.

I said, "Well how are you going to get around? That snow gets deep."

"Oh, we're going to build snowshoes."

When he told me they were going to pull a trailer house up, I said, "You can't get a trailer house up that road with the turns in it."

"Oh yeah? The logging trucks get up it."

"A logging truck's built a lot different from a big long trailer house."

"Oh, we're gonna make it."

"If you get that sucker stuck in the middle of that road next spring, I'm going to bring my tractor up, and I'm going to roll her off the edge and down over that precipice up there on that turn you can't get around. Then the Forest Service'll make you come in and haul it out piece by piece out of the bottom of that canyon."

His jaw dropped open.

I said, "Try it."

He didn't.

Come to find out one of these guys was just out of a state pen somewhere in the Midwest for robbery. I believe one of them there had been behind bars for murder. Two of them were local kids gone bad. They had a woman with them.

After they left I said, "The woman'll kill them. She'll break 'em up before they're done." And she did. They finally broke up over the woman, but not before they had raised marijuana and accidentally sold it to the police in Emmett. There was a big helicopter raid, and it got to be pretty hairy there for a while.

After they had been busted, they left a dirty camp. The next year the Forest Service come by and wanted to know what their camp was like, and I told them it was filthy. Within the week they came back to the camp with a chunky three-legged dog. They went in and cleaned up the camp, bringing out a pickup load of crud.

When we drove back up there, we were pleased to see that the place was clean. They left one light rope strung up, but we cut it down so somebody didn't get hung a-riding. They had been up to no good up there.

We have had a couple of flash floods on Bear Creek, and one of them came in August 1979. Orville and Aloisia had driven in while we were at the tack shed repairing some tack. I heard a roar. The sun was shining, but there had been some black clouds. I said, "There's a flash flood coming." No one believed me.

We ran across the corral and looked at the creek, which was usually dry at that time of the year. Little old Bear Creek was really putting water down, and here came a log, not huge but big enough to go across the culvert five foot wide down at the road. With all the trash piled up on it, I could see that log was going to wash the road out.

As slow as the county was at fixing anything, I knew it would be all year getting a washout fixed. I told Orville, "You hang onto me."

I got out in the creek further than he could safely hang on to me. I kind of sat down and kicked that log loose. The trash was level with the road by then, and the water was ready to go over the top. I almost went into the creek myself. I came within a hair of being sucked down through that culvert. It would have kicked me out the other end before I could have drowned, but it would have been rough going.

We also had some fires. One hot Sunday afternoon we were at the house. We tried to stay around on weekends because of the tourists. We liked to prowl and not take the horses, but just prowl with the pickup. A young fellow drove in and said, "We got a fire."

No matter whether you're sick, tired, or whatever, with the word "Fire!" your adrenaline starts jumping. He said, "It's up the canyon."

We drove up the canyon to get a location so we could call it into the Forest Service. We went down to the Forest Service work camp where there had been men working on survey and other projects, and finally rousted out one guy.

He was fuzzy headed and fumbled around. Finally we got in to the shed where they kept their Smokey (fire) equipment, and we got out pulaskis and a couple of shovels. We got out extra stuff as well because there were other people camping up there who could help work on the fire.

The fire was across the creek and below the campgrounds, apparently from a lightning strike. We took the equipment up and turned our small crew loose on the fire. We said, "We'll go down and call it in."

After a while they came up with compact fire trucks on a three-quarter ton pickup and backpacks to get across the creek.

Once in July of 1979 we were coming back from getting something welded up at Weavers when we saw a big blow-up of smoke out in Crane Creek. We drove up on the ridge and sure enough, there was a big fire going. We drove down off of Dodson Pass and out into all that sagebrush. There they were, ranchers and what have you, leaning on their shovels, and they had a big fire going.

BLM finally pulled in. A Volkswagen van had blown up and set off the fire. A propane bottle that ignited caused the fire, burning a section of land right there.

By August 11 of that year (1979), the Forest Service closed the forest to all chain saws. No cigarettes out of camp grounds, no camp fires out of campgrounds, and they really put a clamp on. And they've done that since, including 1992, when it was so dry.

We had a fire about three or four years ago off the back of the ranch that was started by a lightning strike. Luckily we had company, including Gloria Fasteben from Nampa. We took Wolford's grandson, a big husky fellow, and we sent Wolford out, too. I gave him the coordinates off the map and sent him to Weavers to call the Forest Service.

I told Bob, "You're not coming up to fight fire." He was physically in no shape for that. After he delivered the word at Weavers, and they called it in, Wolford came back and directed them where to go, which road to take and how to get there. We had quite a crew up there before it was done. The state's hot shot crew said they could see the fire blowing up in a fury when they came off the hill at Sage Hen.

I came across the bridge with the four of us on our way to the fire before it had been called in. As I turned toward the bridge, there was a golden eagle sitting on the bridge.As I turned the corner to head north you could see the fire blow up as it hit some bug-killed timber.

I didn't want to go towards the fire, but I knew my ranch, house and all our belongings were at stake. At least we had to try to save the ranch. Two or three lightning strikes were burning together, and we started putting out little fires as we walked up the ridge. Then we did a lot of chainsaw work. By evening it had slowed down a little, and we were able to get three fire lines set up. We were working on the fourth side of the fire when the state hotshot crew come.

Charlie Wallace and Denny Weaver sawed down a monstrous tree that had been struck by lightning. It was four feet across at the butt. It was on fire and dropping hot limbs. The firefighters worked on that fire, including surveillance, for the next four or five days.

Fires in range country are always traumatic because of the cattle, property, timber and lives involved, and the beautiful scenery.

One spring somebody tried to break into the cow camp while I was up there on a field trip with my students from Adrian High School. They tried to break into the salt shed where all the Decker pack saddles were. My principal had helped me bring the kids in, and I sent word back with him to have the school's shop build a foolproof hasp and catch and the whole works like they had built for all my sheds. After we installed those locks there has never been anybody succeed in breaking without taking the whole padlock off.

Once we walked into the cow camp and saw that somebody had jimmied the door and the lock and had kind of torn things up. We had to go back up the house and get our tools, but we patched it up and put it together. For the most part, people left us alone and didn't break in. By and large we were fairly lucky when it came to breaking in and stealing.

One Fourth of July, Si Lett, an old friend who had helped Denny Weaver build his log house, came and put in some new windows in my cabin. The original windows were given to me by Bev Lowe's folks in Wilder, Idaho. I had used them for years. They were windows with panes in them.

Bev Martin's folks gave us sliding aluminum windows that almost fit. Si was from the old school of carpentry, and he wanted to saw it by hand. Everything was measured down to the millimeter, and he spent several days putting the windows in while we ran cattle. He worked by himself a lot of the time.

That same summer we had a get-together with Weavers and the some of the other friends who were there. Si had one more window to put in and it wouldn't quite fit. Keep in mind he was a perfectionist.

I looked at the problem and said, "I can settle that."

"How?"

"Just stand back."

I got my chainsaw, and Si just about had a heart attack. I settled it all right. And when he went to fit the window, it was as if he had done it with the handsaw and the chisel. It was perfect.

What wasn't perfect was what I did next. I set my saw down on the plastic pipe on the water line, and water squirted high as the house. We had to stop and fix that.

One day I had to go to the valley for a doctor's appointment. Bev was hauling hay from Frank Cada's ranch. It was a hot, hot day. She came up over the divide at Dodson Pass and ran out of gas. She switched it over to the other tank, but it had vapor locked although she didn't realize it.

She couldn't get the truck started, so there it sat on a steep hairpin corner while she walked a couple of miles over the hill and down to Dottie Hartgrove's, who took her down to Weavers. Joy came back and was going to see if she couldn't help her get it started. By the time they got to the truck, the vapor lock had gone away, and the engine started.

Robin Stevens rode in on horseback one day. Her father was a rancher at Crane Creek where she grew up. Robin thought nothing of riding her horse out of that awful hot desert and coming in up north and cutting cross country down the road into our place.

She was looking for a place to lay out an endurance ride for an up-coming competition. We chuckled. "How much 'endurance' would you want?" We showed her an easy area or two. She told us she wanted to start further down the mountain where Homer Nesbitt had let them camp in his hay meadows. She started from there and went up over to Tree Spring and out. That's open country, just high desert, rocky and hot, but a good place to start. Then we helped her lay the trail up and on into the timber.

For two years she sponsored that endurance ride. The second year we told her we would help her lay one out and keep it out of the desert if she wanted. She stayed with us a day or two and rode with us running cows. She wasn't thrilled about an endurance ride where we were running cows, and we thought where we took her was pretty civilized.

She didn't think the people who were going on the endurance ride would like to spend much time where we were— every day riding, running cows, pushing them out of the brush, going in through spring holes and across logs, and over old logging trails and up one granite cliff and down another. I don't know what they call "endurance rides." I guess it can't be done pushing a cow tail like a real cowboy.

I was on big Buck, and Bev was on another horse and we were pushing cows up out of the campgrounds and up towards Pole Creek. We were using the road because it was so hot that day.

The Forest Service had a contractor out there, working on grading the road. It was so dry they had a water truck like the loggers use on their roads. He was watering the road so the road grader could roll something besides dust.

A young fellow driving the empty water truck came full blast down the road. He almost ran over me and my expensive horse, which was not mine! When he had filled his diesel tanker with water and started back up the road, he was going considerably slower, but still too fast. I yelled at him to slow down and he did not like it. His return trip was even faster down the mountainside, but this time we were out of his way.

Well, before we got done that day, we met the road grader. The driver was a super nice fellow. He was the owner of the truck and the road grader and was the contractor for the job. We told him our problem and he said, "He's been doing a so-and-so job all day anyway. He's done." He said, "He doesn't have to drive like that. There's no excuse for that." We settled the dust more ways than one on that situation.

People who stayed with us at the Bear Creek ranch put in some long days. We would get in late at night, get up early in the morning and go right back at it again. A favorite saying from a lot of these people was, "It sure didn't take long to stay in this cow camp last night."

One of Bev's favorite sayings, when the nights were short and she was crawling into bed, was, "Better sleep fast tonight, cause it's gonna be a short night."

Another favorite saying was contributed by Orville Harris. A lot of people we visited with on the creek or on the road liked to talk. Orville would say, "He was vaccinated with a phonograph needle."

The second year with the Association we had cattle out on Ola C's allotment because they hadn't put their division fence up.

LaVelle Craig, a permittee, was in, so I asked him, "What's the protocol here? Are we supposed to go out and get those cows and get them in? They won't stay. There's no fence up on the Ola C part."

LaVelle was sitting in an easy chair with a cool glass of lemonade in his hand. He looked over at me with a sly grin and winked. "Well," he said, "feed's pretty good up there, ain't it?"

That's all that was ever said. We didn't go chase them in, Ola C never put their fence up, and we had extra feed. We had so many cows over there I was tempted to go over and place salt tubs. But I didn't think I should push my luck by putting Crane Creek salt on the Ola C allotment.

LaVelle was semiretired, and his middle-aged son Victor was running the ranch. They had one machine break down after another while they were trying to hay.

LaVelle said, "I told my son, if I was working for wages, I would quit."

Victor told him, "If I were paying you wages, I would fire you." And that's how they got along. They got a lot of hay put up and had some humor along with it.

The State of Idaho Fish and Game Department folks knew they were always welcome at my place. If they wanted to ask questions and I knew anything, I would tell them.

I was definitely not in my line of work for the poaching business. In fact, we were in the business to stop the cattle rustling. If a guy was going to poach a deer, he was probably going to shoot a calf right along with it.

One night after being out all day, we drove up the lane a little ways, and there was the Fish and Game pickup pulled up into the brush. The lane has a dog leg you can't see from the road. They were pretty much out of sight from the road, in full uniform. I invited them up on the lawn. They opened the conversation saying something to this effect: "We understand you know everything that goes on here on this mountain, and on this creek."

I laughed and said, "I wish I did."

They were working on information on the illegal hounds and bear hunters. Bear parts were selling for a pretty good price, and they were snaring and running bear with hounds.

I told him a few things and said, "I'll sure be glad to cooperate if I know anything." They gave me their cards. You don't mind working with guys like that. They were gentlemen, and they were doing their duty. Besides, I like to see bear running around and eating up my dead cows.

Another day we come down Third Fork and smelled something dead. We thought it was a dead cow, although we didn't have any cows there. We got out and looked. There was a carcass about fifty feet down over the hill. Bev climbed down the hill, which was as steep as a cow's face. The dead animal was a bear. Illegal hunters had shot it, cut the paws off and took the gall bladder and other parts, leaving no telltale signs behind. The fish and game men came in on that one, but they never solved the case. For weeks it was a stinking mess out there. Nothing smells like a rotten bear carcass, especially if the bear has been eating half-rotten dead cows.

CHAPTER 6

PEOPLE COMING AND GOING

WE OFTEN HAD VISITORS, friends and relatives at our place. Over a ten-day period in June one year we had thirty-three different people visit us! We never knew where our next visitors were coming from. Minnesota or Africa or Canada, a friend of a friend or relative of a friend or relatives of our own, they were always welcome.

Even my eighty-year-old aunt came up. Nothing much slowed her down. She insisted she wanted to run a cow on horseback. So we put her on a horse, and she rode up one hill and down the other, across the creek and through the brush. She had quite a ride for four hours, and we actually found a cow or two.

Sometimes former students or friends would come up and want us to drive their pickup up to Ramage Meadows and drop them to go backpacking. We would pick them up a few days later on Pole Creek where they surfaced after being up at eight thousand feet in the alpine meadows.

One time two of the three students walked in from their backpacking a whole day early. I said, "What are you guys doing in here, and how did you get here?"

"The Forest Service brought us down," one of them said, adding that the forest had been closed because of fire. That was the first I had heard of it.

"Where's Lannie?" I asked.

"Well, when we came out on the road up there, he thought we ought to go left, and us two thought we ought to go right, so we split. We don't know where he is."

We all got in the pickup and started back up the mountain. We drove, and we drove, and we drove. We would see somebody along the road and stop. "Have you seen Lannie, a little short-legged Japanese fellow?" we would ask.

"Nope, haven't seen anybody," they would all say.

We had gone everywhere and were just pulling our hair out, wondering where that kid was. He was only a senior in high school! Then we saw him, out in the middle of the road, saunter-ing along, though pretty sore-footed by then.

"How come you guys came out early?" I prodded. I knew their story wasn't right.

Well, the truth came out. They got spooked up there, and when a kid gets spooked he knows every tree has a cat behind it, and the one that doesn't have a cat behind it has a bear, and the one that doesn't have a bear has a ghost. In that area there was a lot of lodgepole pine and with the evening breezes, those trees rub on each other, screeching and squalling and howling. No wonder they were spooked.

Some of our visitors were especially great to have around. Many of our friends came up to visit and help out, but the ones I'll mention here were on the "honor roll" so to speak. Of course, I don't have room to write about all our favorite people, but here are a few.

Dave and Helen Bivens' daughter Kriss was small but mighty. She was such a good hand with a horse that she could ride any of them. One year she rode with us in a halter top, mind you, and a cap. It's rough going in the hawthorne brush, and she began to look like it, all scratched up and sunburned! She was tough and would eat anything. How many junior high school kids will eat beet greens? "I'll eat about anything if you give me soy sauce," she said, so she got it.

Kriss came for a week, several summers. Even though we told her to stay with us when riding, she knew the country so well it was no big deal if she got side-trailed or bush-wacked. We knew she could get home or come up the road until she found us.

Once Kriss knew where she was going with her horse and where the cattle ought to be, we could turn her loose. If it were possible for anyone to get them there, she would.

One day Bev, Kriss and I had been driving cattle, and at Woodard Camp, the buggers split into two groups. I went through the campgrounds lickety split, through the creek and a fisher-man's camp, straight up a ridge behind chasing those cows. I yelled at them so much I was hoarse.

Bev took off the opposite direction, yelling and chasing. About twenty minutes later Kriss came riding back through the campground. "Have you seen any cowboys?" she asked the fisherman.

"Yes, young lady. In fact your dad went east up that mountain, and your mom went across the road and then west."

She informed him about who was her mom and dad and who wasn't!

My friend Mary Awohi, right out of vet school, came up to ride with us. We had been riding all day when she picked her horse's foot up to see why he was limping. A loose horse shoe nail caught her just right and ripped her finger open. I never saw anybody so green and pale as she got. She nearly fainted right there—a veterinarian who can take care of any guts and gore!

"I can't stand much human blood," she said.

"Dr. Shultz" took her to the house, put her on the davenport, covered her up, elevated the right parts and got her finger in a bowl of epsom salts, as she instructed. We got her patched up, but I still chuckle thinking about how shocky she got over such an injury.

The guest who stayed the longest at any one time was my old college classmate, Bev Olson, M.D., an emergency room physician. She spent a month with us the first time she came, and we had a lot of fun. I hadn't seen her since she was a medical school student in northern Italy eight years before. I was heading for central Africa to see my sister and her family. I met Bev in Rome, and she showed me a few things most tourists don't get to see. Now it was my turn.

She had never been to the ranch and thought our area was magnificent. We were clearing trails up in the Pole Creek area when she looked down the canyon at the wild and beautiful raging stream, evergreens and brush, and said, "You mean you get paid for this? You ought to have to pay them to be able to work in scenery like this, and good fishing and good hunting besides. I can't believe it!"

I just laughed and said, "You'll change before the month's up!"

Sure enough, before she went home, she was sure we were not getting paid enough for what we were doing, even if the scenery was great.

The next day she got to practice her emergency medicine. We had porcupine quills to pull and an old mare to clean up after she had foaled the night before. A couple of days later the cattle came in, and she rode and worked eleven hours alongside us. She was a real trooper and got to be a pretty good hand with a horse besides.

One time while Bev was helping us round up some cows her horse turned in back of a cow. About that time the old cow urinated down the front of her boot and pant leg. She laughed it off. "Pee is benign," she said, and went on her way. I still laugh about that.

Late one evening we were prowling for rustlers and doing other night-time work. About 11 o'clock we saw a porcupine a mile or so from the cabin. Those animals are a real nuisance, so when he went up a tree and I couldn't get at him with a shovel, I asked Olson if she would mind getting out of the pickup and holding him up the tree with a shovel while we drove home to get the gun. So she waited there bravely for us. It was a perfect setup for a snipe hunt, but I didn't want to wreck her morale because we had a lot more work to do!

Olson was always taking pictures. Dave Bivens took her with him to the front of the cattle drive so she got pictures of more than green rear ends. Her favorite saying was, "I don't take pictures of sunrises, just sunsets. Most people can't tell the difference anyway!"

After a cold wet day, the dogs were in the house. Olson was roasting a weenie in the fireplace and dropped it. She picked it up. Dog hairs! The good doctor said, "Oh, heck, I'll just roast the dog hairs off the weenie. I don't believe in the germ theory when I'm on holiday."

One of the best Kodak picture-perfect moments when Doc Olson was with us was the day a wood cutter got hurt.

The story began for us when grizzled old Butch (the rider who followed us working for the Association) clatter-banged up in a ton truck. Blood was running down his face. He was coming unglued and couldn't get out of the vehicle. "Get me out of here! Get me out of here!"

He was frantic and claustrophobic. The pickup had broken windows, and the door wouldn't open. He had to herd the old thing, and he didn't have matches to light a cigarette. He was frustrated.

We got him out, thinking he was really hurt bad. Instead he told us about the woodcutter who had felled a tree on himself three miles east of Woodard Camp. Butch had been driving cattle by when he saw some little kids crying, "Our daddy's hurt bad. Please help us!"

Butch tied up his horse, left his dogs, somehow hot-wired the hurt guy's truck (there were no keys) and found us.

Doc grabbed her black bag, and we snatched up other first aid supplies. I took Butch with me in my pickup, and Bev Martin took Doc Olson in hers. (Butch hadn't had a bath in a while; it was the kindest thing I could do for my partners.)

When we got to the scene there were three dirty little kids and a big pile of wood. A guy was lying on his belly on a thick foam mattress, smoking a cigarette, covered with a sleeping bag. A Forest Service man was there looking worried.

Butch told him, "She's a doctor."

The Forest Service guy let out a big sigh and got out of the way. He sure didn't want to practice first aid!

I walked up to the man on the mattress and told him the lady was an emergency room doctor and to level with her. Doc did not look like a doctor in her cowboy boots, Levis and Stetson, that is for sure, and he was reluctant.

I wish I'd had a camera while she examined that fellow. Crusty old Butch (with his five-day-old beard, clothes he had worn all week, rough and rumbly) was kneeling beside spiffy little Doc Olson. The contrast was so sharp I could hardly keep from laughing out loud.

Old Butch was the nicest guy with a heart of gold. But his pickup, his person and his life were held together with baling wire and twine and tobacco juice. His tires were so bad he carried two spares with him all the time. He was a grimy pot-bellied old cowboy; Olson looked like she was from an *Urban Cowboy* fashion magazine!

Butch dug out his jackknife and handed it to Doc so she could cut off the guy's shirt. She didn't flinch.

We eventually got the guy in the back of a pickup on his way to the hospital, and his kids got rides down the canyon. Turned out he had only broken a few ribs and was bruised and sore, but nothing serious.

Bev and I were both first-aid instructors, and our "education" came in handy one August evening. We had just gone down to the corral to feed the horses, and two pickups went by lickety split. We both said, "There's gonna be a wreck before they get done."

About an hour later, one of the pickups came back up our lane. The people in it were frantic, wanting to use the phone. The other pickup, they told us, had gone over the road, dropped down over the creek, and rolled three times. One of the young men who had been in the rolled pickup seemed to be OK, He said, "Yeah, my uncle, he's all right, but my aunt, she's not too good."

We didn't have a phone, so Bev took one of the boys to Weaver's, trying all the while to get someone on her CB. I took some blankets and big bath towels to bind the lady because they said her shoulder hurt her. I went to the wreck with the nephew.

They had hauled the woman up the bank, steeper than a cow's face, probably seventy-five feet, and laid her in the barrow pit. It had been so hot that day that she was not dressed for the cool night. They had her lying on a thin camper pad of some sort and were going to leave her there until the ambulance came. I tried to convince them that as far as that ambulance had to go to reach us, she should be put in the back of the pickup and taken to the house. Her husband would have nothing of it.

Finally, I got her husband off to the side and told him what was going to happen to his wife if she lay there another three hours. "She could be hurt internally, and there are no ifs, ands, or buts about it. We are gonna put her in my pickup, and we are gonna mosey back to my house!"

At the house we built up the fire, wrapped up her shoulder again, and treated her for shock. She was in a lot of pain. They drank all our cold water and smoked until we could hardly see the ceiling. They were nervous. The older man, the father of this uncle, kept saying, "I gotta go back to that wreck and get the rest of my beer, get the rest of my whiskey!"

I said, "You're gonna what?"

He said it again, so I told him, "You're not going anywhere. You've already had too much," and wouldn't let him go.

Well, the Ola ambulance started our direction, threw a tie rod on their vehicle and had to radio Emmett for another ambulance. The Emmett service was broken down, so the deputy and three ambulance people arrived at our place in the deputy's pickup.

About midnight the Gem County sheriff and an ambulance arrived together, lights all going. You would have thought we were in downtown Boise with all the emergency lights going up there in the timber! Thank goodness, no sirens.

By this time, by actual count, there were nineteen people in the hundred yards from the gate to the fireplace; the lane was completely filled up, and our two stock dogs wanted to bite them all.

By this time her arm was swelling to the point I thought her humerus was probably broken. They got an air splint on her, and by 12:30 they were loading her. Everyone finally left and we got to bed at 1:30 a.m. I couldn't sleep.

We were up at 7 a.m. and went to the wreck. There were three unopened twelve-packs of Coors and empty cans in the cab and all the way down the hill. At least no one was in their pickup camper, or they would have been killed for sure; it was stick kindling. The woman was lucky to have only a broken scapula, humerus, and a disjointed shoulder.

We helped quite a few people through the years. Most of them wanted to pay us, but we didn't take anything—except one time, and I didn't feel bad about that at all!

On our way back from a trip to town, around 9:30 at night, we saw a young fellow hoofing it down the road. He flagged us down.

We picked him up, and he told us that he and another fellow were stuck in the mud with two small cars. Listening to him, we figured out about where they were and knew it was bad news. I really didn't want to go there, but I didn't want to keep him all night, either! He helped us feed the horses and unload the pickup. We took our flashlights, got back in the pickup, and started up the creek. It was a sea of slime. It had been raining something awful, three-quarters of an inch the night before!

It was pitch dark. The dust had been eighteen inches deep on the logging road before the rain, and now had turned to slime. I chained up my big outfit, and after a long time we managed to finally get one rig pulled out. The other kid must have thought we were going to leave him and not come back. He drove out of the mud and followed us out in his car. The ruts on the road seemed bottomless, and there were rocks and limbs in the ruts. I don't know how he did it.

I was glad the second guy got scared enough to get out of there on his own. When he offered us some money, I took it. We had used a lot of gas and I was so fed up with that mess. I never felt bad about taking his money.

One day after we had been on horseback running cattle and packing salt all day long, a guy came by on his little Honda 90. He said, "I need a saw. A tree fell across my road into camp and none of us can get out."

"Where are you?" I asked.

"Well, I'm up to Rammage Meadows." That was ten miles away.

"Yeah, you wait until we get done here and we'll come up and do it. I know where you're at, so take your bike and get going and we'll be there." I don't loan my saw to people I don't know!

A large lodgepole had fallen across the only entryway into that big campground, and no one could get out! We sawed that green log out, threw as much as we could haul onto our pickup and brought it home for wood the following year.

Some of our drives were to get the cattle up the mountain further for feed, but other times we were gathering them up to go to a sale. In the middle of August one year Bivens said, "I want a truckload of cattle. Get me a semi load off of this area." I was sure we didn't have that many cattle of his on the place, but we did manage to round up eighteen.

When the big semi truck came, we loaded the eighteen head of Bar-Eleven cows (a brand) from the allotment. Then we put on the stragglers we had rounded up with Bivens's cows. We told the truck driver to follow us up the canyon eleven miles and we would dump the extra cows out. The driver wisely wanted to know how he was going to get turned around up there.

I said, "If you can get to where we want you to go, there's room to turn around."

I assured him that logging trucks come and go on these roads all the time. He looked at me kind of funny, crawled into his cab and away we went. This driver was a great big fellow, and his wife was with him for the ride.

The rest of us in the pickups drove on ahead of the semi on the mountain road so that we could stop a logging truck if we saw one. The road was too narrow for passing. We finally parked and waited for the semi to catch up. We waited, and we waited. No semi!

By the time the truck finally came, the driver's wife was a nervous wreck. She got out of that truck swearing, screaming, yelling at him and at us and at the world in general. When she finally calmed down a little, she said, "I'll tell you, we were comin' up that road, and I looked back in the mirror and the set of duals'd be hangin' off over nothin' and I think, 'I'm gonna jump.' I look out, and it's two hundred feet down to the creek." It was probably only a hundred, but so what if you're going to jump!

She continued. "I wore out one rosary comin' up here. I'd reach over and beat on my husband and scream at him."

One snowy evening we were coming around Second Fork and got down to the bottom of the hill, and there was a pickup with California license plates sitting there. We stopped and asked if they needed help. Obviously they did. One of them said, "Yeah, I've tried to get up this hill three times, and I can't make it."

Somebody else asked when the snow plow would come by.

I said, "Maybe next week if you're lucky." We could not get them up the hill, until I finally I put everybody in the back of their pickup, and I sat in front with the driver and told him how to drive.

One night about nine o'clock the sheriff's deputies drove in, looking for information about a man and his wife in their forties. The deputies thought the couple was camping at Pole Creek. The man's dad, once the game warden, was with the sheriff, and I felt sorry for him. He was getting' up in years.

The couple was supposed to be home at four o'clock the day before and never showed up. I told them where I thought that pickup had been sitting, and it was right were I said, near the springs right out of the Woodard Camp area.

The dad said, "He's supposed to be up to Pole Creek."

I said, "I don't think so."

They had been looking since 2 a.m. the morning before, and this was at about 9 o'clock at night. They had been all over those new logging roads and the old man was getting frantic. I couldn't blame him.

This was the same fellow we got quite a kick out of another time. He was always fishing. The old fellow was a fun guy to visit with. One day I was horseback when I met him on the road towards Pole Creek. I said, "Where you been?" We had not seen him all summer.

He said, "Well, I had a wreck and my wife got both her hind legs busted, and she's just now getting around." They were in their eighties.

Once we were running cattle up the creek, and the camps were full even though it was during the week. Woodard Camp had several campers in it with their tailgates to the south. One camper had its door wide open. It was a low-slung pickup.

A big old Hereford bull with large horns peeled off the road on that little two-bit mule trail there, and got down in around the campers. I could see it was trouble in the making so I peeled right after him on a wild horse. That old bull looked at me, and then he looked at those campers. He decided that the campers were the lesser of two evils, I guess, and he took off in their direction.

About then somebody opened a camper door, and that blocked his way. He had to go to the left, and when he did, there was another camper door open that was a little bigger than most. I thought for sure he was going to run right in and load up. I knew he was going to wreck the whole works! At the last second something detoured him. He shook the camper as he went by and kept going.

A couple of days later, the camper came and introduced himself as a friend of my late father. We were visiting, and he said, "You know, I don't know who it was, but there was sure some good cowboying going on up the creek the other night!"

I said, "Oh." I dreaded what I was going to hear.

"Yeah, there was an old bull come in there and I thought he was going to come right in my camper," he said, "but that cowboy poppin' his whip and his dogs was a-working good. He could really handle that horse, and boy, there was some good cowboying going on. I don't know who that guy was, but he was doin' a good job."

I just laughed and said, "I think you're lookin' at that guy.'"

Old Roy about died. He had no idea that we were cowboying or that it was us in the middle of his camp making a mess.

Neither one of us minded if we were mistaken for men sometimes! In fact there were times we would suck in our chest and stick out our gut and TRY to pass for a man when we would get in a camp of long-haired hippies. It could get scary sometimes with some of those characters. We usually kept a whip in our hand.

One day we unloaded, and there were cattle in the campgrounds. I started toward a camp. My dog Shorty wasn't behaving and took off. I yelled at him, "Here, Shorty! Here, Shorty! Get back here! Back!"

A fellow sitting in an old-time canvas sling lawn chair turned around and looked at me, his fist doubled up. I noticed that he was a very short man and figured he must have thought I was calling him "Shorty."

He was about ready to sit up and teach me a few manners right then and there! Just then my dog showed up. Lucky me!

I put Old Buck, the big buckskin, down a steep bank, but the cattle got in such thick brush that I couldn't get him through it. I got off and put the reins over the saddle horn and thought he would stay—he had before—but the old poop decided he would get back up on the road. I was in the thorn brush so deep I couldn't get out.

I just let him go. "I'll have to walk home," I thought. It was only about two miles, but with spurs a-dragging and batwing chaps a-flapping, that wasn't going to be sweet.

About the time the old horse hit the road up above, here came a car, and I thought "He'll scare the livin' daylights out of Old Buck, and he'll jump that cattle guard down there with my good saddle on him and be long gone!"

The horse went down the road and kept going. I ran the cows out of the brush and picked up my hat that the horse had tromped. Still looking for Old Buck, I got back on the road and walked around the corner with my batwings a-flopping and my spurs a-dragging in the dirt.

There they were. The driver of the car had caught Old Buck and was waiting for me.

"I thought I recognized that horse," he said.

He was one of the straw bosses with the loggers. He asked if I had been hurt or something.

"No," I said. We got to visiting.

One of the first things he said was, "Why are you and your cows in the middle of my loggin' crews?" He didn't like the fact that we had cattle around and they kind of had to watch out for them while falling timber.

I turned it around and said, "Why are you and your loggers in the middle of all my cows?" And then I saw the hostility melt away. He could see both edges of that sword.

I said, "You gotta blame the Forest Service for this one, because we are locked in the books every other year. We're on this side of the allotment this year and on the other side next year. You guys have five years to harvest any timber sale, and you didn't have to be over here this year. So maybe you need to talk to the Forest Service."

Ever after that we were good friends. One time one of my horses threw a shoe way up the canyon. Some of his men were coming down for something and he said, "You take Carol clear to camp, and don't come back till you get her there."

I appreciated that. Later I brought the truck and picked up my horse that didn't have a shoe on.

After that he would shut off the machinery when we would come by him with cattle on the road. And that meant sometimes shutting down everything and everybody. The loggers would just shake their heads.

On our side, we would try to run the big drives after they had quit at five-thirty or six. That would put us clear til midnight getting home some nights, but it was worth it.

One day we had driven a lot of cattle up Third Fork and then took them up Mesa Creek on a logging road. We kicked them off into another big canyon. On the way back we rode home on a new logging road that came out just above the main forest service road going up the creek.

We could hear a horn honking and people slapping the side of a pickup, making a big bang, and dogs a-barking and kids a-yelling. We got where we could look down through the timber, about a hundred feet straight above them.

They couldn't see us, and they were driving some of our cattle that we had driven the day before going east. Here they were, bringing them back west and running the living daylights out of them.

I waited until they got right under me and then bellowed in the deepest voice I could muster—"LEAVE MY COWS ALONE!" It must have been like God Himself "talking" to them.

With no idea of where that voice come from, they yelled at the kids to quit banging the door and shifted their rig into high gear and took off in a big cloud of dust. I laughed all the way home.

The woodcutters were irritating as well as fun to watch. One fellow was notable. He was cutting up garbage wood, a pile of white fir that had been cut for road right-of-way about five years before. White fir isn't any good two minutes after it's cut. That wood had been in our way for a long time driving cows, and I always told Bev I was going to cut a trail through it. I told him, "Boy that looks like good easy wood. If you don't get that cut up and loaded, I will. You better take it all."

And he just grinned and said, "Yeah, I know that's good wood. It's good and heavy." Well it was wet as all get out, he took her all, and the mess was gone.

Another time there was a huge yellow pine out on the edge of a kind of a cliff above the road, and we came around there with a pickup one day and heard a saw. When we got to it, Bev and I looked up and saw a guy cutting a huge tree. He had an old saw, and it sounded kind of drastic, so we drove on down out of the way to a point where we could watch what was going on, and not get took with that tree. He sounded like an amateur!

After a while his saw stopped, and I heard him yell to some-body, "Bring me an ax!" The tree was probably close to four foot through at the butt, and I don't know what he was going to do with an ax, maybe cut his finger off. He eventually did get the tree down, but it was plumb dark by the time he got it. Most of it went on over the cliff, and he lost it anyway.

We often had trouble getting our cattle through woodcutters if they wouldn't shut their chain saws off. One day they were cut-ting up a big tree, and we came up the trail from below them with cattle. The cattle would not go by. I rode over to them and yelled at them, and they just looked at me and kept cutting. So I yelled at them again and motioned to them to quit. I yelled at them a third time and made a motion of slitting my throat; then they got the message.

My old college classmate from Colorado, Betty Crow, was riding with us, and Betty said, "Well, one look at you and they would do whatever you want." I had forgotten about my broken crooked nose, two black eyes and a big old scab on my nose. I was a sight for sore eyes.

CHAPTER 7

WILD ANIMALS

ONE DAY WE SAW A BEAR that was so big he could pull a good-sized dead hereford cow along with one arm. The bear reached over with a front paw and spiked the cow's shoulder, dug his claws into the muscle, picked up the front end of that cow and slid her along wherever he wanted, just like you would reach out and grab a little lap dog by the scruff of the neck and throw it around. We wanted the tag off that cow, but Bev and I decided we would collect that tag on the way home if that bear was gone! I didn't need a tag that bad.

Another time after school started and we were gone, our friend Doc Hyde came up. He parked at the corrals, put his horse in the corral, fed it, and crawled in the back of his pickup with the Redbone hounds he had been running. His dogs were restless all night.

At the crack of dawn, he got up and turned his dogs loose, to get them limbered up, and he went to saddle his horse. The old horse's head was up and looking east over the corral, and the dogs were beginning to have a fit.

He told me later, "I was trying to put the bridle on Old Joe, and I couldn't get it on her. I picked up my ears and looked over there and followed where she was looking. There was a monstrous black bear."

He got his gear together right quick, but the dogs had already hit that bear, and it took off to the south towards the log bridge over by the rock house. Doc ran that distance with his horse, and the old bear hit the bridge and went back north again and then up straight east through my fence with a bang, the dogs right on him. On he went. He got in a draw and up a scrawny pine tree.

Doc had friends who were supposed to meet him on Third Fork, so he left his dogs there to keep the bear up the tree and rode the mile or two see if they had arrived. When he came back without them, he waited. The bear came out of the tree. The dogs couldn't hold it.

That bear come right for Doc, so Doc shot him and shot him again, and the old bear just flinched and kept coming. The dogs started chewing on him so hard that he stopped to swat at the dogs, which gave Doc a chance to reposition and reload his gun. The bear went up another tree where he was finally shot dead. I was kind of glad to see him end up in a rug. We had bear visits all summer at the cabin corrals.

Our first two years were the worst for porcupines, and we learned to kill all we could find. They were pests!

We had a haphazard cowboy biffy on the back of the tack shed with no door. The porcupines had a heyday in there! They love plywood, maybe the glue in it, because they'll eat up signs and empty salt tub bottoms we just put out the day before. We finally had to put a makeshift door on the outhouse just to keep them out.

They loved chewing on tires, not just on the salt tubs, but the ones still attached to our vehicles!

They could give quills away, too. One night we were in the pickup we found one of our horses so afflicted. It was common practice for us to leave the horses out on the road, for there was a mile of road, fenced on both sides, with my property on both sides of it and a lot of grass. We were driving down the road and Bev said, "Wait a minute. Back up. I think Dink has quills." We backed up, and he had a bunch of quills, a sight to behold! We got over twenty quills from that horse's nose.

We figured out the only way to take them out is to use pliers and pull the worst quills first, before Dink got too punchy. When he started getting wild, I put on a leather glove, rubbed him up between his eyes or up under his forelock, and then came down on his face talking to him; at the same time I grabbed two or three quills with my fingers.

Misty, an unexpected buckskin colt, was several months old when she confronted a porcupine. We had been out working hard all day, and came back in the evening to find that colt with quills in it. It took us almost an hour to fix her up, and she had over twenty quills. Some people call it "porkypine poisoning."

The quills didn't just stick on the horses. One day we were saddled up ready to go, and Jiggs came around from the other side of the corral with porcupine quills in his nose. Everything came to a complete a standstill. I got hold of the dog and right quick grabbed those quills in about two swipes.

We saw a heifer that belonged to Bivens with quite a few quills, so we called Dave, who sent out the foreman and his righthand man. We chased that heifer over about two hundred acres worth of pasture. Once she was roped and stretched out between two horses, we all worked together. We pulled fifty-three quills out of her face! She looked like she'd had grains of rice thrown at her. A lot of the wounds were badly infected, the pus was running, and she was pretty smelly, but she survived.

If you ever get bored with life, try skinning a porcupine, whether you want to mount him taxidermy style or not. Don't get in a hurry, and don't worry how you do it! It's a challenge to try to keep the quills from falling out. Quite a few of them will anyway.

Another time, two years later, we were driving the pickup up the Third Fork road, and the biggest skunk I have ever seen was walking up that road. He KNEW he owned the road and let us know that he wasn't in any hurry to get out of the way of any little red pickup. We decided we weren't in too big of a hurry, either, and waited for him to get out of our way.

On an August night in 1977 our dog was barking something awful. Finally Bev and I got up, took the pistol and went on up behind the woodshed about fifty yards into the forest. We saw a skunk in the light of our flashlight!

The greatest skunk memory I have, though, happened about two o'clock in the morning when all our doors were wide open. The worst noise, just frantic, came from the woodshed by the house where our dog Shorty slept.

I thought, "What in the world?" About then, the smell hit in the house. The skunk must have come into that woodshed, and since Shorty did not take any "friends" to bed with him, he must have protested.

The skunk sprayed Shorty's head and the wood around. By the time I got out there the skunk was long gone, but he sure left his smell. We built fires in both fireplaces to get some air circulating, opened up all the windows and of course the doors were already opened up.

We tried everything on that dog, and finally we got down to tomato paste and tomato sauce out of the cupboard that we made pizza and spaghetti with, putting that on Shorty's head to wipe the smell off. That worked better than anything we had tried, and the poor dog began to think he might live. The dog and the entryway stunk for quite a while.

I will never forget the evening we saw the Great Horned Owls. We had been out prowling under a full moon. We thought we heard something at the lower cattle guard, south of the house, so we stopped, listening. We could hear Great Horned Owls calling to each other, "Oooooooooooo, who who! Who?"

We came to a stop and just watched for a while. We could see the outline of an owl at the top of a tree just south of us, right smack into that big full moon. I couldn't have drawn a better outline of him filling the moon with his "ears" sticking up. Once in a while he would flap a wing, calling to his friends, one on my left and one on my right. It was fantastic.

There was many a night at Bear Creek that we would hear these owls calling all hours of the night. I loved to hear those big owls so much that I got so I could talk to them and get them to talk back to me. Early one spring when we were coming in here with the snowmobiles with some friends of ours, I was walking along the road on the hard packed snowmobile tracks calling to an owl. I could hear him flying and following me in the timber, about fifty yards to the west of me, and just flying along and talking to me. I would talk back to him as I walked, and pretty quick he would fly. He could see me, I'm sure; I never did see him. As long as I kept talking to him, he kept coming right along, and I really got a kick out of that.

There were always great horned owls in the timber just north of the cow camp corrals. That was an easy place to hear them calling and see them on their nests, bringing food in the evening to their young. They are neat critters.

We were always seeing deer, in the corrals, deer in the yard and the garden, eating it up, deer in the driveway. This was common. Several times they were spectacular.

Our first year we seemed to run into three or four light-colored deer with large spots on them, like a pinto horse, lighter in color. One of them was albino, with pink, glassy eyes, pink-ish ears, and a very light nose. There wasn't a black or dark spot on his head or muzzle where you would usually see it.

That same year, coming back down the road towards Bear Creek, we looked off to the left over a big embankment into Squaw Creek where there is a nice green meadow with brush on each side and a long island in the middle of it. There stood a big four-point buck. His antlers went straight out past his ears and then up, a true trophy deer. He just stood there and watched us. It was fantastic. We have never forgotten that.

Another time we were rattling along up the road in my old pickup when three deer scrambled out of the creek. The bank was so steep, if they hadn't been so scared by my noisy pickup, there would have been no way for them to get out. They went straight up that bank, graceful as they went.

One time we saw about eighteen or twenty cow elk and as many calves walking up the edge of the mountain. They weren't scared; they knew they were safe.

Another time right up on Third Fork ridge we turned the horses to go over to the salt lick. The dogs started having a fit, and out come an old cow elk, snorting and really on the prod. I was beginning to wonder what was going to happen! Then along came an elk calf. I was leading Ace, my good cutting horse, who was also packing salt, and was I glad it was him!

The elk calf came right up to him, thinking it was his mother and trying to find a place to nurse. Kind of hard on a gelding pack horse, but Ace just stood there. I was afraid we were going to have a first-class wreck with that old cow. I guess she was a little bit scared of the dogs, too. Eventually the calf wandered off, and they went their way.

The next time this happened, we got pictures.

We saw a Pileated Woodpecker on top of the Loop Road one time. I had been hearing them, a very distinctive call like six Redshafted Flickers put together. One day we were lucky enough to see one. We heard and saw a few more later. They're about as big and black as a crow except the males have a red cockade on the back of their head. Getting to see something this rare was gratifying.

Even the insects could be interesting. We would find a hatch on the creek and watch the fish rise to them. For several years at certain places, we would find the most fantastic ladybug hatch. They would migrate down the canyon, come out by the corrals and keep going to who knows where. Some years we saw them half way to Pole Creek. The air would be orange with them! Apparently they came up from the valley to the mountain to propagate for two or three years in a row, and just seem to disappear.

One fine evening we were sitting outdoors enjoying a visit with my mother and Alice Ritter, a family friend. All of a sudden we heard a noise in the timber at the edge of the yard in back of the house. There was a chipmunk frantically going up a pine tree; we couldn't figure out what his big toot was. When he was up the tree about twenty feet, a weasel came up the same tree from the ground.

That chipmunk went like he had his afterburners on. He got up as far as he could go in that tree, and the weasel was right behind him. The chipmunk jumped and landed about four feet away in the branches of another tree and started down that tree, just a chipping, and that weasel flew right behind him. By the time that chipmunk hit the ground, the weasel had him. That's how fast he was. I couldn't believe my eyes, it was so amazing.

Sometimes we caught fish rather unexpectedly. One time the water wasn't running in the house at breakfast time, so I walked the line up Bear Creek, taking joints and reducers apart. At the reducer that went from the inch and a quarter down to one-inch I found where the trouble was.

A trout eight and a half inches long had come down the pipe. When he got into that reducer, half of him was into the reducer and half of him wasn't. He was a fierce-looking critter, but he tasted pretty good, even if he had lost some of his girth.

Sometimes we would throw a bucket into Bear Creek to get water from off the bridge, and there would be a fish in the bucket. Easy fishing.

One year we had coyotes in the Third Fork Pocket that looked an awful lot like old Jiggs, my big blueheeler dog. It was fun to watch them. They would follow along behind us as we were running and rounding up cows, walking right behind our dog that was walking behind our horse that was walking behind the cow. Then my dog would chase the coyote. The coyote would get ahead and then turn around and chase the dogs back to the horse. After a few weeks of this, they seemed to have reached a truce.

One coyote in particular would go out there with Jiggs and act like he wanted to learn how to heel a cow or he would sit on a little knob or on a rock howling. I rode as close as twenty-five feet from him, and could see the very light pink in the roof of his mouth, big long fangs and pretty white teeth. He just howled at us and talked to us, giving us a lot of shows for three seasons, until somebody apparently got him in the fall, and we never saw him again.

When any of my friends came up to go hunting, they knew not to shoot the coyotes. We didn't have too many, and they were real helpers, catching mice and squirrels and grasshoppers. I valued them and liked to see my coyotes around. They never bothered my cows or calves.

One time we were coming home from up around the Loop Road, and there was a bobcat out in the middle of a clear cut area.

Another time, on a field trip with biology kids, a bobcat jumped out and barreled right down the middle of the road in front of the school van. Bobcats often came through behind the house at Bear Creek, looking for something to eat, and they would come back out of my pastures with squirrels in their mouths. I valued them highly because they ate "tons" of squirrels.

My friend Bev Olson came out here for a month our second year. My partner Bev Martin had gone to the valley for supplies, and Dr. Bev and I were holding down the fort. We were down at the corrals and a lady in a big Suburban slid to a stop, and half frantic called to us, "Do you have a gun? I need a gun!"

I wasn't about to give a gun to somebody as haywire as she seemed to be! I finally got it out of her why she wanted a gun.

She and her husband had been coming down the creek about three miles north of Bear Creek, and they had hit a cougar. In broad daylight he had jumped out from the creek side and onto the road in front of that big old Suburban. He had rolled and tumbled the full length of that Chevy. When he got up he was dragging a hind leg and was scarred up, so her husband stayed to watch him, while she left to find a gun.

I told her all I had was a .22 rifle, but I would go get it, and we would come back up. I went up to the house and got the rifle, put the dogs in the pickup and away we went. When we got up there, the husband said, "That cougar was sitting right there for quite awhile, and he's dragged himself back into the brush. I think we need to do something."

The cougar was in the campground areas, so Dr. Bev and I took Jiggs and we went back and forth, back and forth, looking for a sign, looking for blood, looking for a cat in ambush, whatever it was. Old Jiggs did not like it. He would go around for a ways, get the scent of the cougar, and come back and sit on our feet.

It was kind of weird to be out there hunting a cougar with a .22 rifle and a blue heeler that was scared! Just the same, I felt obligated since he was right there on the creek where we had cattle, and a wounded cougar would help himself to a calf or a camper's kid.

We scrounged around quite a distance from where he had been hit. We could not find him. Finally I told Bev, "If that cat is good enough to crawl beyond a half a mile radius, I don't need him." I figured that if a cat has nine lives, he had probably used seven of them that day when he got drug under the vehicle for about sixteen feet and rolled and tumbled under that big machine. I often wondered about that cougar.

About three o'clock in the morning one year—a week before school started—I heard an ungodly screech, squall, and holler right beside the house. It sounded like a fingernail scratching the blackboard while chewing tin foil on a tooth filling. My old dog came crawling out of the recliner and sneaking up to the bedroom, shivering and shaking. He didn't want anything to do with it. Definitely a cougar.

The rattlesnakes we found were usually less than three feet long. But they were broad, good for belts and hat bands. We killed them whenever we got the chance; their bite was no good for us humans, and it certainly wasn't good for the cattle we were taking care of.

Our first year a friend killed a two-foot rattlesnake with about eight rattles by our gate. About six weeks later Bev and I heard a snake buzzing while we were walking down to the corrals one evening to feed. We both took a double-take! We looked everywhere, and finally found that snake under a little pine tree.

Another time I was fixing a cross fence when from out of nowhere slithered a huge three-foot long rattlesnake with twelve or fifteen rattles on him. I stopped dead in my tracks! He quickly hid in a brush pile and started buzzing me. I was not going in after him!

A little later that year in that same area we were leading pack horses with salt. I was riding Smokey when a big snake came out across the road. Old Smokey had been bitten by a rattlesnake before and tried to buck. He swapped ends so fast that the lead rope got under his tail, which he does not like. I don't know how I stayed on him!

I discovered one day that the rattlesnakes "liked" my three-quarter ton Chevy pickup with dual-glass pack pipes. As we went across a bridge near where we had seen snakes I goosed it to go up the hill. The pipes cracked, and I heard a rattlesnake buzzing. I thought, "Hmmm. I wonder if I can do that again." And got the same results. Apparently they could feel the vibration.

Another time on Third Fork I was driving my Datsun, which was showing some signs of aging, and we saw a snake going across the road. I thought, "Well, I'll finish you off!" and ran over him. But he was still crawling, so I backed up and rolled over him again. I thought he was finished. I turned off the pickup and started to get out when I heard him start rattling. I thought "Holy Toledo! Where is that snake?" I was afraid to get out since I didn't know where he was and the dumb pickup wouldn't start. It (the pickup) was deader than a doornail. I finally rolled it down hill to start it, and that tough snake had crawled off the road.

That same year one cold morning late in August we were out riding and took a short cut. I felt Buck step down when he went into a hole, but he just kept going. Bev came along behind and hollered, "Hey! Do all snakes have flat heads?"

I whipped around and said, "What do you mean?"

She said, "I think that's a rattlesnake and Buck just stepped on him." That snake had been curled up in a ground squirrel hole for the night. It was so cold the snake hadn't moved anywhere. Bev piled off of her horse, got a stick and finished him off after a chase. I don't know how that snake could go so fast on a cold morning.

CHAPTER 8

HORSES WORKED FOR THEIR HAY

IN THE NINE YEARS WE WORKED on The Mountain, there were twenty-six horses we worked seriously. We had some excellent ones (others couldn't have been more eggheaded). Some years we had as many as sixteen or eighteen horses scattered around. People would bring them in and say, "If you want 'em, use 'em." And sometimes we would. We usually kept about eight on tap, fed them grain and hay and kept them up. At the end of the summer, their owners would come get them. We didn't keep many horses over the winter.

Bev and I each needed three horses, two good saddle horses and a pack horse. When we packed a horse it carried salt, salt tubs, a chainsaw or whatever equipment we needed for salting, clearing trail or the like. Some horses were used for both riding and packing. We had our favorites. Ideally each horse would work one day out of three so they could rest up. When they were used two days in a row, they were dead tired by the end of the second day! Sometimes we would ride each horse for part of a day, using all three horses that day.

Most of our horses were hard working, hardened, and used to the altitude. The country was rugged, rough, rocky, brushy with downed timber, granite, and lots of open rock patches. On that terrain, ride a green horse three or four days in a row, and it would be broke of too much bucking.

Before we rode some of the horses that were brought in, we would acclimate them to the weather, altitude and night noises (or lack of noise, depending on where they came from). There was only one horse we sent back without even riding once. He was too wild and wouldn't settle down.

Each horse saddled differently. Some of them didn't care if you took the saddle, threw it at them, cinched them up rough and climbed on. But for others, like Dutch, one of our best horses, we took our time and got it right, because we had a lot of miles to go. We always used a curry comb and scrubbed out the blanket after every ride because pine cones and thorns and pine needles would get under it. We wore out blankets that way, but we didn't care because the horses didn't get sores.

We knew good equipment was important. A lot of our horse equipment was custom made. My Uncle John Henderson used to own a ranch in Round Valley by Donnelly, Idaho, and later taught me how to braid rawhide, and I made our tack for all the horses.

In the tack shed we used horseshoes for bridle and rope hangers. The shoes were welded up and nailed to the walls. Each horse had his name over his hanger, his own set of reins and rommel, a bit with headstall, a bosal or halter, so anybody riding with us could find what a particular horse needed. This also kept from passing disease back and forth between the horses because each had his own set of tack.

Most of the equipment was rawhide, as I was learning to work and braid rawhide from my uncle John. We had as many as ten full sets of rawhide: reins, rommels, bosals, headstalls, hanging at any one time. Each bosal had its own fifteen-foot lead rope, and it was always on a horse's neck, with a bosal under the bridle. Packhorses usually had a halter with a twenty-foot lead rope tied around his neck.

Our friends at the Adrian High School shop welded together two saddle racks that held three saddles each and bolted onto the back wall. That kept our pack and riding saddles off the floor and out of the way. We also had steel holders for two-by-fours to make a double drying rack, eight foot long. I put it under the eaves by the open window for drying wet saddle blankets. Later the high schoolers built three large steel mouse-proof boxes to store stuff in. We used the boxes for our dry saddle blankets, some of our work horse collars, our rain coats and this kind of thing.

I did most of the horseshoeing myself. I learned that craft partly by watching commercial farriers and cowboys, but mostly from the college of hard knocks. The first time I actually shod a horse years ago I was so unsure about my shoe job that I hauled along extra shoes, nails and a hammer! The shoes all stayed on, all the way up through the shale and the granite and the downed timber. After that I shod my own horses unless I was physically unable. Some years I would put on sixty or more shoes on various horses.

Carol doing the hardest job of all—shoeing horses.

Bev's favorite horse was a beautiful sorrel quarter horse. Rosie's owners advertised her in the paper as a parade horse. I told Bev I didn't think a valley horse of that caliber would be able to work in the hills very well.

We went to see her, and the folks told us they had used her in the hills hunting. To prove it they took her out on a big ditch bank that hadn't had water in it yet, and rode her into the ditch and back up out of it. We were impressed. Rosie was well-mannered, well-trained and sure-footed. I think it kept my more cautious partner out of some of the trouble I would get in from being on the green horses. Bev rode Rosie for a long time.

Rosie did have one bad habit, though. She could open gates. One day she got into the oats by opening the gate, and I found her there the next morning, one sick horse. The vet came up and worked on her, but she was sick for a week or two.

Wouldn't you know, as soon as we put her back in the corral, she went directly to the gate and started nosing at it again! We had already put a chain around the gate so there was no way she would get into the oats again.

Horses are like people or chickens or anything else: they each have a personality and a pecking order. Ace ruled the roost that first year, and he was the best cutting horse I ever owned. I could show him a cow out in the middle of nowhere on this mountainous 26,000 acre allotment, and he could cut her out without reins.

At first he wasn't as eager about packing salt, but he was a fighter! One night Ace put another horse over a three-wire fence with a foot to clear, and that horse just kept going. I found him in the third pasture.

A year later the son of a wild horse from the Owyhees in Southwest Idaho came up. His name was Tuffy. He ruled them all, including Ace. It was unbelievable. He would just walk in, and the rest of the horses gave way to him. I never saw him fight or kick unless he had to defend himself, but he ruled the roost, no doubt about it.

Ginger was a spoiled nuisance, a handful. (See "The Strawberry Roan" in the cowboy poetry section.) Tuffy and Ace would take turns running her out of her feed bunk, kicking and nipping at her. Ginger would take that for about two weeks, and then she would start in on them. She would beat the snot out of whichever gelding was handy and rule the roost for about two weeks. Then one of the geldings would start in again, and he would rule the roost for about two weeks. That's the way it went.

One day we came home from riding and found Ginger had put Bev's appaloosa gelding, Dink, through the steel gate. Ginger had pushed a twelve-inch diameter post nailed solid with five cedar poles on it out of the way and had sprung the gate. All the horses were on the road. She was mean enough she could hold her own.

Ace was the only horse that started and finished our nine years with us. He was broken down and out to pasture by the end, but was with us nonetheless.

Getting Ace to pack in the beginning was hard work. We were packing salt with Jake and Ace. Jake was an excellent pack horse, as calm as a lap dog. He had done this before. We could turn Jake loose when we were clear up on Green Field flats, and he would follow us home.

One day we decided it was time for Ace to learn how to pack salt. So, by hook or by crook, we got two hundred pounds of salt on Ace, loaded up Jake, and started up the lane out of the cow camp to get on the main forest service road. Ace was not happy.

By the time we hit the Forest Service road, about a hundred yards from where we had put the pack on, Ace threw a whamdinger of a fit. One fifty-pound sack went flying through the air past me like a guided missile and landed in the weeds in the edge of the road. That loosened everything up, and before we got him calmed down, all four sacks, two hundred pounds, were lying all over the road, the lane, the weeds and the trees. When we got him tamed down, I gave him a little motherly advice cowboy fashion, loaded him up again, and that was the last unprovoked whamding he ever threw packing.

He did throw one more fit packing salt, on Wilson Mountain, but this time I thought he was justified.

I was riding Gigi, my little half-Arab mare and leading Ace with a load of about two hundred pounds. We had been following fresh bear sign, and Ace was fine. We got up out of the timber and into the tall grass and lupines, which were full bloom, perfume that you couldn't believe.

All of a sudden he just went crazy! He went around me, and I couldn't hold him. I couldn't hand the rope around my body fast enough for the circles he was going, bucking, snorting, and blowing snot.

Nothing came off his load, surprisingly, but the saddle began to slip. Here I was, on the mountain by myself, trying to keep from getting tangled up, and trying not to turn him loose. All of a sudden the saddle slipped and went clear under his belly, load and all. That poor old devil came to a dead stop, I was sure he was hurting, his back was swaybacked like an old horse that had been mistreated.

That took the fire out of the old buzzard. Somehow I got those tight straps undone, reloaded him, and we went on to the last salt ground a hundred and fifty yards away.

Best I could figure, he must have either seen or smelled the bear I kept seeing signs of. Ace was raised with bears at my uncle's ranch, so he would have known about one.

Ace packed pretty good for us, but never completely lost his reluctance. Sometimes we would take three or four loads a day with the horses from where we had dumped salt off with the pickup. Ace would haul the first load cheerfully. The second load he was not very happy with—but he would go even if he did not like it. The third load was almost impossible if we didn't feed him some oats first. There never was a fourth load for Ace! He could count and knew when his day was over!

When Tuffy came to our "slave" job, he hadn't lived a hard life. Our friend Denny Weaver hunted with him and that was about it. We had to teach him to pack. That wasn't the hard part; he didn't mind carrying a load. He did not want to lead with it.

The second time we tried packing Tuffy, we were going up Third Fork Ridge, which is pretty steep and rocky. He started balking, so I put Bev behind him with a stock whip. Every time Tuffy would quit, he was popped, and after a while he got the idea that it was nicer to walk forward. Then to register his complaint he started bucking. We were about halfway up the ridge and on the steepest part! Somehow I managed to keep him going up the hill. He bucked with two hundred pounds of salt all the way to the top of the hill.

Normally we would walk, rest, walk, rest, until we were all the way up. But he bucked all the way. We made good time that day! After that he settled down and began to pack pretty good.

When Tuffy would pack, no matter where it was or how inconvenient it was, if he felt that pack begin to slip the least bit, he would come to a sliding halt. He didn't care if I had to climb a tree to get around him and fix the problem. He was not going to move! I learned to just get off and fix it, because I was going to drag him if I didn't. This was good in a way; he didn't take off bucking like some of the other horses we had when their packs got loose.

One time we were coming through granite where another horse almost pushed me over the cliff, Tuffy's pack slipped a little. He could have made it on down through the stairsteps, but no, he had to stop. I had to climb up and around, hang out over nothing by my shirt tail, and finally got where I could put that pack back on him.

Some of our remuda was easy to shoe, but others made up for all those combined. Ginger was a roan appaloosa with a wild temper a fast kick and a mean eye—but she was tough as whang leather!

Before I bought her, the farrier could not shoe her until he threw her and tied her feet together. She had never been shod free-standing, so she had to learn how to balance that long lean body of hers. Then she really became hard to shoe!

We found out she shod best when Bev would gently pet her head and face and talk in monotone to her. There were times when even that didn't make any difference! Bev would say "Move!" and then Whamo! Sometimes I didn't move fast enough. Ginger could kick, and I would roll across the corral in the dust and manure. One time she gave me a double kick and broke the shoeing hammer handle so hard that the head flew out of the corral! We found that head months later in a post pile we were cleaning up.

One day I was shoeing a front foot. She looked around at me, rolled that eye, and the next thing I knew she had picked up her back foot and kicked my hat off, let it roll back under her and stepped on it. What a character.

When this old reprobate met her untimely death, I cut her shoes off (I had just put them on two or three days before) and made a couple sets of bookends out of them. They're reminders of many fun but hard times, and frustrating times with Ginger.

The strawberry roan was a hard old rip to saddle. She had been a kid's horse and was spoiled rotten. Up here it took two of us to get a saddle on her at first. And then when I got on her, she would go backward as fast as she would go forward. In time she turned out to be a great horse.

The first year I had Ginger we were up on Buck Mountain and had taken an old logging road. We had always wondered where it went and decided to ride it out that day. We had chased a bunch of cattle in there, and we thought if cattle could go, we could.

Before long we came to the end of the road. The mountain was pretty steep there, so I told Bev, "Well, this is the end of the road. Instead of riding back, let's just cut straight down the mountain and hit the main creek. It's gotta be within three miles of us or less."

She wasn't too gung-ho about the idea. I guess I liked to cut across country and make my own trail to see how big a mess I could get into. She had more sense. I went first. In three steps I was in a mess. The slash pile looked pretty benign, but it was deep. The front feet of that old mare weren't touching ground at all and we were hung up with her belly on the slash pile. "How in the thunder am I going to get out of here?" I thought. The mountain was steep.

That mare was so ornery she managed to kick and break things until we finally staggered on down the mountain with the slash. Bev came around a different way.

On another day we were going up Third Fork, and I raced up the ridge on that roan after some cattle that had gotten away from us. Ginger hit sheet lava that was hiding under knee-high grass. Neither one of us saw it. We slipped and went down, right to the edge of a good drop-off! Her left front and back leg were swinging back and forth. I didn't know how we were going to get out of the mess.

I thought, "If I unload, I'll tip her over, and she'll land on me. If I wait, how is she going to get up with just two legs touching solid earth?"

I didn't have a whole lot of time to act, for all of a sudden she gave a lurch and came up on those two right legs, bringing me, the saddle and herself all up at once on that slick basalt rock. She made a big jump and landed down below it, and we just kept going. She was as nonchalant as anything; I was white knuckled!

Once we came down off of a ridge together driving cattle. Bev had started to yell, "Don't come," but it was too late; we had already started over that road cut.

I soon knew why Bev said not to go that way. It was so steep my feet in the stirrups were up even with Ginger's ears, and my hat was hitting her rump from leaning back in the saddle so far to keep us balanced. She was having trouble with control even then. She hooked a log lying half buried in the dirt with her hind leg. That slowed us down! But instead of panicking, she brought that log along with her and used it as a brake all the way down.

I had a lot of respect for that horse after several escapades. Bev rode her one day over some stuff she normally wouldn't have tackled with the horses she usually rode. I had just ridden down a slash-filled slope and was calling to her, "There's just one way. Come down over it!"

Photo by John Blackmer, Idaho Statesman

Carol on Dutch, Bev on Ginger in Miner's Flats.

Bev and Ginger had a safe descent, and then Bev told me, "Now I know how you can go in some of the places that are impossible for normal people to go. You ride this old mare!" What a horse!

Roany was a great big chunky quarter horse. We didn't use him very often because he was about twenty-three by the time he came up, but sometimes we needed an extra horse. He had done a lot of packing, and he could pack a big load. He wasn't afraid to work.

His problem was that he was so big that as much as he had done this job, he would still hit trees! It didn't matter where we were—lodgepole, firs, yellow pines, or sagebrush—he had hit them with those packs. And he would groan, it hurt so bad. Up and down Bear Creek canyon, up and down Pole Creek canyon, Squaw Creek canyon, there are scars along the trail on trees where old Roany hit them and just kept going.

Dusty was a buckskin mare we bought from a friend who did a little speculating in the horse market. We bought her, wintered her over, and brought her up the next spring. She had put on a little weight on good feed but not anything out of the ordinary. The first week in June we noticed her bag was beginning to fill a little with milk.

On June ninth we packed her for the first time, and for never having packed anything, she did all right, though she seemed a little lazy. We packed her again up Third Fork ridge and around. She always wanted to lie down when Bev was leading her. Two days after our salting was done, Bev went down to feed, and there was a little palomino Appaloosa colt with Dusty. No wonder she wanted to lie down and get rid of that two hundred pounds of pack! We named her colt Misty.

The next year Dusty was still lazy but definitely not pregnant. She would kick the fence with her back feet until they were swelled up, sore and beat. She knew she wouldn't have to work then. We still packed her, whether she liked it or not, but her days were numbered.

Bev was riding Dusty and leading Ace packing salt to the top of Greenfield. Dusty started side-stepping. Somehow she had gotten the rope under her tail and did not like it. The more she crow-hopped, the more that rope tightened. She clamped her tail down and then started bucking. Bev stuck with her; it was a pretty good show.

Finally Bev gave the rope a big jerk as the mare was whipping around and got it out from under her tail. Dusty was up in arms by then, so Bev and I traded horses. What a ride! We went out in the middle of the meadow, and she bucked so hard that I lost my hat. I was determined to ride it out. When she wanted to quit, I would hit her with the spurs and over and under the romal, and we would go for another big swing. We tore around that meadow, up one hill and down another and through the meadows and through the timber. I think we were both having fun.

One day we started on a trail-clearing, trail-marking expedition to the top of the mountain. Bev was riding Dusty and packing Ace again. Old Dusty went all right, but no ball of fire. When Dusty started getting ornery, I said, "Tomorrow we'll pack that knuckle hold, and you ride Ace home." Ace was a good saddle horse.

We had two pack horses that trip, because we were cleaning trail also. We camped overnight and did a little fishing at the headwaters.

The next morning it took both of us to get the pack saddle on her, a pretty scrappy fight at that. We put all the camp on her—two chainsaws, the gas, the oil, all our cooking utensils, our ax for cleaning and marking trail, the paint, anything and everything—and we started down the hill.

I was riding my favorite little Arab, Gigi, probably only two-thirds the size of Dusty. When I felt a tug on the rope, I looked around just in time to see Dusty, pack and all, standing and rearing on her back feet. She was coming toward me, pawing with her steel shoes in the air, and squealing like an old stud. She could have killed me! Gigi saw Dusty and side-stepped just in time, and the old rip hit the ground a pretty hard jolt. Then that feisty critter came back up and tried again! I said, "That's it. This old gal is going to the sale, packers or whatever."

I got her reined in and imparted a little school marm knowledge. We got down in the canyon, and she came skidding off the granite, trying to rear at me again. She hit the back of my horse, almost knocking us over the cliff! No doubts in my mind now. I told Bev, "This horse is going for sure. She just about killed me!"

When we got back I called the friend who sold her to us, and said, "Let's find a market for this turkey. She's going." He sold her to another horse trader who tried to sell her to a sheep outfit, but the boss found out who'd had that horse. He said, "If Carol and Bev can't handle that horse, I haven't got a sheepherder that would even come close to handling it. I don't want her."

She ended up in eastern Idaho somewhere, I don't really care where she ended up—dogfood or feed for the tigers in the Portland Zoo. She was bad news on this mountain!

One of the better pack animals we used was a little white mule named Molly, who might have weighed seven hundred and fifty pounds soaking wet. She could pack about anything we wanted to put on her, and she pulled real easy, she never tightened the rope up.

We packed salt on her sometimes, but if we were cleaning trail, she was the pack animal for that. I rode her little friend Toby, a chocolate-colored mule about the same size. We could clean a lot of trail.

Snip was a horse I bought from a friend in Oregon. She came from some of the best cutting horse blood in the Northwest. I thought she would make a good cowhorse.

She was a good size for me, a chunky little horse, easy to get on, and easy tempered. She learned how to pack quickly, and was a great pack horse. We would pack camp on her; we would pack a little salt on her, and she was good to ride. But the day I got her up to a bunch of cattle, I found out that genetics doesn't mean everything.

I was watching the cow instead of her, and she piled me into a mess of rocks. She definitely did not want to work cows and made no bones about it! Kriss Bivens riding with me saw me fly off Snip. "You went so high I had time to see where you were going to land, and I saw the rocks, and I wondered how I was going to haul you out of there!"

Snip was a fighter. One day I turned her and two other mares out behind the house. They were fighting, and then I heard a sound like a metal baseball bat hitting a power pole as hard as a kid could swing it, then splintering. One of those mares had kicked Snip in the stifle and broke her leg, and that was the end of the fight. I had to put her down.

We packed several times for the Forest Service. One time we packed a heavy water box when they were developing a spring toward the top of Bear Creek Canyon. Having us pack it was an easy way for them to get it up there, and we didn't mind, because our cattle were using that spring.

That box was a two-foot cube made out of steel and was heavier than sin. Also there was a great big roll of used one and a half-inch pipe higher than my head, and I'm five feet, six inches. I wondered how I was going get that three miles up Bear Creek!

We decided to pack all this stuff on Tuffy. We put the steel box on Tuffy's left side—which was the uphill side. The tall roll of pipe we hung on the right side—which was the downhill side most of the way. I put one hundred pounds of salt on the pipe side for ballast, tied it all down tight, and we went up the trail.

Believe it or not, we did pretty well. Tuffy watched the trees. When we got in tight places, I would stop my horse. He would back up and shift his weight a little and move his shoulder to get that thing by. He seemed to realize that the black plastic pipe might break if it was hit too hard.

Another load we hauled was about as tough. The roadless area up on Green Field flats was a problem because people were still driving up there, and there were no signs to tell them not to. The Forest Service asked us if we would take up a load of fence-posts, signs and equipment for them.

The fenceposts were four-by-fours about ten feet long. Even after I cut off a couple feet, they were still longer than Tuffy! The signs were heavy steel about two by three feet and said "Road-

Bev Martin on appy Dink leading appy Ace on the south end of our allotment in Green Field Flats. Ace is packing salt and an empty salt tub tire.

less" and "No Vehicles Allowed." We had a big pack. Tuffy was loaded to the limit, trying to wheel in and out of the lodgepoles and such.

As we went along, we proclaimed the area "roadless" by throwing signs and posts along the way. Along came two people, a man and his wife, on two little Honda motorcycle-type things. She had a poodle of some type in a little basket on the back of her little Honda. We were packing "No Vehicle" signs, and here they came right toward us. I took their picture.

While on our way to rebuild a fence on the mountain, we decided to salt the cattle. The Forest Service had dropped fencing supplies by helicopter, and we had five-hundred pounds of salt by the radar dome on Snowbank Mountain. The next day we started from home at 5:30 in the morning, salting all the way up the canyon to the dome.

The radar dome is a significant place for tourists. This time I swear they were all waiting for us. There was a swarm of people, all with cameras, Easterners and Southerners in their fine-feathered best and floppy hats, oohhing and aahhing. We went behind a rock pile to try to load the horses. People were trying to hold our horses for us, kids petting them. That old mare of mine hated kids, and she would just as soon kick a head off anyone as look at them. I finally got after one of the kids so bad that they all pulled back and left us alone.

The problem was that we had two horses and five hundred pounds of salt. This was not nifty since it is a lot of weight on each horse, the load shifts around and we were going downhill!

I told Bev, "I hope to thunder this stuff hangs on until we get around the corner and down under this big snow cornice that sticks out over there!" A huge drift fifty or sixty feet deep was sticking out along the trail, and if we could get behind it the tourists couldn't see us anymore!

We loaded up and got on the horses, and the cameras were going crazy. I suppose we ended up plastered all over the United States in pictures. We did make it around the hill and started under that big snow cornice and into a swampy area, when, sure enough, old Ace's pack slipped. I wasn't surprised!

When we got back to the cabin, it was ninety-eight degrees on the porch. That is hot for this country and set a record.

What a day.

CHAPTER 9

TOURISTS—GOOD, BAD, INDIFFERENT

WE HAD ONE TOURIST on the creek for parts of several years. The first year we saw him, he was in a homemade camper outfit. He had a bunch of kids and a wife.

He had dogged some cattle off the creek on a hot afternoon. We drove by looking to see where we were going to work the next morning. As we drove back down the creek, he rushed out to the road. It scared us half to death. He had hip waders on, a sidearm, a fillet knife, and a .30-.30 in his hand. He was wearing an old straw hat and a shirt unbuttoned to the belt, with a scar from neck to navel. He had a skinny little kid or two with him. We decided we had better get to know him a little better so we stopped and persuaded him that he really probably didn't need to be packing a .30-.30 around because it wasn't that wild here, contrary to what he might of heard.

He would camp for two weeks at a time. Ever after when we rode by with the horses or slowly drove by with the pickup, he would rush out to the road and say, "They were up that way!" or "They're up east of me, up in the timber." Later on, we saw him with some sneakers on that hardly had anything over his feet, just hanging on with baling twine. The hotter it got, the less clothes he had on. We would see him way up in the timber, miles up the mountain from camp, and he always had at least one of his kids with him. They had just been up there hiking, looking around. He had gotten rid of his gun finally, but then it got hot, and he was hotter, and he had even less on than before. He started wearing shorts that looked like somebody's lace curtain out of a bedroom or living room, and that's all he had on. It didn't take much imagination to know that. You never knew where you were going to meet that wild man, but he was interesting.

One time we had ridden all day and worked hard. We had just gotten to the house when a pickup came whizzing by with a poor muffler. The driver slammed the brakes on, backed up to the corral and there they were, looking over the corral at the horses and the tack shed.

Needless to say, I jumped right on them and wanted to know what in the world they thought they were doing, because I didn't like the looks of them or the way they acted. They gave me a cock and bull story that didn't check out when we drove up the road later that same night. We got a license plate and some other things on them.

Another time, on my birthday, I had busted some ribs riding up top in the Green Field Flat area. At 3 the next morning, the dogs started yapping and wouldn't quit. Somebody had drifted in. You could hear the pickup coast down the hill into our corral area on the main road and stopped. The dogs were so loud that they backed up the road and into my lane, and in the headlights you could see three heads silhouetted. They turned around and went on up the road, kind of slowly. They sounded like they had glass pack mufflers. Looked like a poaching outfit to me. Who needs that kind of thing in your lane or in your corrals at 3 o'clock in the morning when you have a tack shed full of equipment and good horses there? I think they were casing the outfit and thought maybe nobody was home that late in August because we were probably in school.

There was one night, after we had worked hard all day driving a lot of cattle, when we finally got to bed real late and been there just long enough to drop off. About midnight, the dogs started having a fit. We had horses grazing on the road, so we didn't think too much about it, but they just kept it up. Pretty soon, we woke up enough to realize those were people yodels, not animal yodels coming out of the dogs.

Right quick we threw on some boots and got up where we could look down to the corrals, and there were flashlights. Boy, the adrenaline gives you a shot then, and your hair kind of stands up a little. We grabbed some guns and flashlights, and Bev went down the lane as a decoy. I tiptoed down past the rawhide shack, through a little meadow pasture and came in behind them.

Of course, they didn't know I was anywhere around until I hollered at them. You can really throw the fear into folks catching them off guard that way. All of a sudden, they're looking down a flashlight with a gun not aimed at them but knowing it could be in a split second. They were the fellows with the dump truck and the small lowboy that would haul a backhoe. Another little self-loading truck had been up the creek for three or four days loading wood, but they didn't seem to be doing much. I wondered then if they weren't poaching or rustling cattle, and I still think maybe they were. Anyway, they didn't get treated too kindly for stopping at our corrals at midnight and being in the corral over towards the tack shed. We won't go into details, but I never saw them again. We got license numbers, names and what have you. One of my business friends in the valley said later, "Yeah, I know one of those guys, and he's pretty shaky. Watch him."

After the treatment he got, he was smart if he never did come back again because it was going to get a little hotter if he did. We did not appreciate midnight, 3 a.m. or even 10 p.m. guests in the corral.

One evening it was just dusk, and the horses were acting up in the corral. We had ridden hard that day, so they should have been so pooped they couldn't do anything. Then the dogs started barking. We slipped down, and again I took the gun and went through the pasture where they couldn't see me coming. Bev went down the lane where she had cover and some room to maneuver. It was so dark down there we really couldn't see much, but we could see two bodies leaning on the corral across the road from the tack shed corrals. I hollered real gruffly at them, and they turned around and about melted into their boots. Then I saw they were women.

They had come up from the guard station where they were working for the Forest Service. They had been through there in the daytime, had seen the horses, and wanted to come up and pet them. We visited with them and tried to assure them that if they would come in the daytime or earlier in the evening and let us know they were there, they were plenty welcome. We weren't there to throw the fear into them under those circumstances. We never did see those ladies again.

A Forest Service employee at a lake not too far from there visited with Bob Wolford, a friend of mine. Bob said, "I'm going to pull my boat over on Third Fork and leave it."

This Forest Service employee asks, "Well, where in the world are you going to leave it over there?"

Bob told him and he spit out: "Man, I wouldn't leave it there. I hear them women are pretty rough and tough. They'll not take any garbage off of anybody. You might not have a boat left." Of course, Wolford just chuckled and never bothered to enlighten him. He knew some of our night-time escapades at those corrals.

One summer the Forest Service had a crew working up on top of Loop Road. One of them was a young man who liked to "run" things, although he was just a peon on the crew. I was riding Big Buck, the kind of horse that when he got out of the truck you hoped you had a logging road somewhere that you could just let him out and run for a mile, maybe two, just as hard as he wanted to run. Then he would calm down and could work some cows. This young man had seen me do it the day before, and this time he got to where he could really watch what was going on. When he heard me pounding down that dirt logging road on 1600 pounds of galloping horse, he climbed up onto a stump right quick to get out of the way. As I whipped by him in a blur, I heard him say, "Your cattle went THATAWAY!" He looked like a little tin soldier sitting up there.

Another time we were driving cattle up the creek. We picked a bunch up out of the campgrounds. Just past Woodard Camp, going east toward Pole Creek. I thought, "Boy, here we've almost got it made for easy getaways for these rene-gades." Around the corner came a small station wagon. The driver pulled over in the barrow pit because we had quite a bunch of wild cattle, but he wouldn't shut his motor off. He might as well have come through the cows if he wasn't going to shut his engine off.

The cattle split. Some of them went up an almost impossi-ble steep bank, and some of them then went back on the road. Bev went back on the road with them to try and salvage that bunch. I hit the spurs to my horse and went straight up that mountainside where those cattle had gone. It took about a half mile run to get around them in the timber, the brush, the rocks and the steep mountainside, but I did get around them, and they came back the same way.

I could hear Bev's whip popping and her saying things and yelling, trying to get her cattle past that car. The driver still wouldn't turn his engine off. I heard her yell at him two or three times, "Shut your engine off!" He wouldn't.

I thought, "I'll teach you."

In the back seat were two middle-school aged kids. The wife was on my side of the car and the husband on the driver's side, which put him towards the middle of the road. Bev was trying to dog the cows past him. My cattle were stampeding, just flying and thinking nothing of going back over that cliff we had all come up. Some of them wanted to go to the front of the car and into Bev's mess. I dogged and headed them and made them go back down the cliff. The lady and kids looked up in time to see those cattle coming, and her face told it all.

I yelled hard at her to shut that engine off. Her husband just got down and looked under the steering wheel at me and shook his head.

I yelled again to shut that engine off, and he wouldn't do it. I made a "slit your throat" gesture and shoved those cattle right down on top of him. His wife reached over and grabbed the keys out of the ignition, and the kids started rolling up windows. Rocks were rolling. The cattle stayed more or less on their feet, leaning back on their butts and sliding down that cliff. They engulfed that little station wagon. I came right behind them on my horse.

The car wasn't damaged, but the mentality of the people inside was. I'll bet the next time that old boy will think about shutting his engine off, and I'll bet he doesn't ever forget that.

By then Bev's cows could see mine going around the car, and they beelined by it. All we did was knock his mirrors around. He should have been thankful that was all that got knocked around.

Up towards Pole Creek there are some flats in there but no campgrounds along the road. Somebody had made a staircase with logs down off of the road and cut a trail down to the creek onto the flats, and had made kind of a permanent camp in there.

The man who built the camp always drove a new, small pickup, polished and fancy. It was pretty nice. He had a big German shepherd, and he seemed to think he owned the country.

We would come through with cattle; he would just let the dog go. The dog would have a heyday. We couldn't catch up with him with the whip because we would scatter the cattle. After about three times of that, we asked him to please keep his dog with him at least, but he didn't care. Obviously, he was one of these guys who thought cattle didn't belong where he was.

One day the cattle we had rounded up were tired, and so were we. I remembered that "ecologist" camp, and I said, "Let's turn them right here." We turned the cattle and pushed them over the edge of the hill on his wooden steps and put them down in and around his campground. Feed was good, partner, but the smell was going to be even better. After they stayed there a day or two, he could burn cow chips and wouldn't have to cut wood.

Every time after that when we came by, I never said anything to him, but he would hold onto that dog. He would see us coming down the road and he would be in the pickup with that dog in front. The dog would lunge out the window and bark at the cows. He would grab that dog, stop his pickup and shut it off. Then he would put his arm around the dog's neck and his hand on his muzzle. I guess we made a believer out of him.

One late afternoon we were coming up the creek with horses, looking for cattle. We parked down on the other side on the school section and rode over the little pass. Bev could hear cattle up above the road on the west side, so she went that way.

I went down through the campgrounds on old Ginger, my strawberry roan, a wild-looking horse. There were campers, but it was awful quiet. I rode through several camps—not a soul in sight. I could hear Bev with the cattle. I knew I had to be at a certain camp to head them off when they hit the road, so I hurried on and started out of the creek to come up through this one campground.

A big camper was pulled in there with the curtains drawn and the door shut. It was pretty warm. I could see they had probably been out swimming or fishing. They had jeans strung on the line, and there was a barbecue sitting there and some used tinfoil and stuff. I rode through it and went up on the road. There were no cows. I rode down the road a little bit—no cows.

I could hear them up in the timber yet, so I rode back down towards that camp. Right about then, here came some cows behind me. They rumbled past me like a dose of salts and went right through that camp.

The people at the camp were young, probably high school kids, and by then they had gotten curious. Apparently they had seen me ride through, and they came out of the camper, thinking nobody was around. I doubled back and started down the grade. The girl was outside with not one stitch on in broad evening light, and here I came.

She thought I was a fellow, and she did a fantastic quicky cover-up job with used and smoky tin foil. She slapped each side of her chest and across the lower middle section with a piece of blackened foil, and with that outfit she probably had more coverage than she'd had all day. The tin foil bra and G-string took the cake because they came right off the warm barbecue, were blackened and well used.

It was hilarious, but I had to chase cows. I couldn't stay and give her a bad time.

I told Bev afterwards, "If I was a fella, I'd never get off of this creek. There's so many interesting things going on."

Another batch of tourists that got more than they bargained for were camped at Woodard one summer. They had a baby playpen set up with netting on it and a baby in it, and their camp chairs set up. After they had been there a day or two, we drove up the creek with the truck and the horses to see what cows were there. We told them we would be bringing some cows up, and they might come through camp, and they probably better move the playpen and make sure the baby was safe. Where it was sitting, we told them, was a bad situation because if the cattle got on that side of the creek, they would go through that playpen.

They moved it a little bit. An hour or so later we got our cattle up there, and they split. Bev was on the west side, and I was on the east side of the creek. We had quite a drive going. Some of the cattle that had been on the creek didn't want to leave and were fighting the idea. We finally got most of them over on Bev's side of the creek, but I still had two or three on my side. When they got to Woodard Camp, they peeled off that cutbank, hit the creek flying, and headed for that camp.

I just had time to scream, "Watch out!" They grabbed the baby, somebody grabbed the playpen and jerked it, and a cow went straight between them and headed out. I was right behind her and got her turned again, and she went back in the creek and the brush.

We had come right up the creek in all that brush and water and all those rocks, and that pulls horseshoes off, but I was determined to get her. She was an old Black Angus, and nasty tempered. When she got back in the creek again, she didn't figure I would follow because it was so brushy I held onto my hat and went through that thorn brush and stayed right on her, my blood flowing freely from all the scratches and digs.

We went another hundred yards in that horrible brush and up the creek, dogs barking, the whip popping when we got out of the brush a little, that old cow bellering and bawling and me yelling at her. It must have sounded terrific with four horseshoes in all those rocks as background sound.

My horse and I went on around the corner, and she tried to knock the horse down into the creek and then got on an island. I got up on it and tried to move her out of the campgrounds, but she wouldn't move. I was getting ready to get off the island and looked across the creek. There was Lady Godiva herself. The brush was pulled back, and just her head and her chest were sticking out. She didn't have a stitch on, just long hair dangling. She had two little kids that acted like little cubs, sticking their noses through the brush to see what the noise was. I was bleeding from one end to the other with thorn brush scratches all over my face and neck and arms. I looked like I had been in a first class tomcat fight.

I yelled at her to get out of there and stay out and don't come near it. "That cow'll take ya," I said. "You probably just better get back to camp."

I had to ride up the creek quite a ways and then through some brush to get onto dry land. I rode through their area to see them busily throwing camp together in the back of the pickup and getting out of there. That was probably a wise thing, because that old cow was really on the prod. When they saw me up close, they looked at me like they had seen the devil himself, I was bloody from one end to the other.

Late one evening, we were down towards the Forest Service ranger station chasing renegade cows that were giving us fits. You couldn't get them any other time but right at dusk, when they had come out of the brush. If you tried getting over there early in the morning to catch them, they would hightail it into the brush.

They were giving us a hard time. Bev had some cattle in the brush above the logging road and I was down below it digging them out with the dogs and yelling at them. The dogs were heeling the cows, and the cows were going from one big brush pile to the next, thrashing and bellering.

When we finally got them out I was down on the creek, right behind the guard station. There's a huge hole there where the kids the government hires to work in the summer like to swim. I didn't know anybody was around there, or I could have had a little fun. The next day we were riding up Third Fork ridge looking for other cattle, and we came across some government workers, some college kids, and the Forest Service surveyor. We visited with them a little bit. They had been in the deep brush surveying all day, so I thought if there were any cattle down in that big draw, they would know it.

We asked them if they had seen any cows and one of the kids looked up and said, "How many cows are you missing?"

With a straight face, I said, "Oh, about five hundred."

He couldn't believe we could have had that many cows to start with, much less that we would be missing that many and how were we going to find them in this "godforsaken country," as he called it. We told him we thought we could probably handle it. The girl had been real quiet up until now, but then she said, "Were you two down at the guard station last night getting cattle out of the brush?"

I said, "Yeah, right on the creek,"

"I was skinny dippin' and I heard what I thought was two cowboys chasing cattle. My clothes were on the other side of the creek and I didn't have time to get over there. Here came one of these guys on horseback with his dogs, and the cattle ahead of him. I didn't know if I was going to live long enough to find my clothes. I'm really relieved that you two women were doing it instead of the two men that I thought were there."

We chuckled about that. It would be perfectly normal for her to think I was a fellow, with a Stetson pulled down over my eyebrows, boots and spurs and a pair of heavy chaps. Besides, your voice gets hoarse after a while yelling at those cattle.

At that time (1977), few women were out there doing that job. It was no wonder people thought we were men, and it was probably safer in the long run that they did think so.

CHAPTER 10

MY BROKEN NOSE AND OTHER ACCIDENTS

WITH THE KIND OF COUNTRY we were in, the kind of horses we rode on, and the kind of job we were doing, we would get bucked off, knocked off and rolled on once in a while. I always seemed to be riding a horse that wasn't broke very well. I sent my good Arab, Skipper, to a trainer to teach him to stand still so this old lady could get on him! When I went to pick him up six weeks later, the trainer told me, "If you are the least bit scared of him, haul him to town and get rid of him." I hauled him to Bear Creek.

The next day we were headed out to run cattle on Third Fork ridge. We were going down the road, and he was just stepping right out and doing well. I was impressed. He was a fast walker. He still had the habit of flexing his neck, throwing his head back toward the rider. He must have caught me bending over a little because he hit my nose and busted it.

Boom! Blood squirted everywhere. My quick movement in reaction must have scared him. He bucked me off onto the top of a ten-foot pine tree which I kind of slid down, and he took off for home.

Bev took off after him. I got up, dizzy, and felt my face. I didn't have a nose! It was laid over on my cheek like a bloody marshmallow. Being a first aid instructor, I knew I would never make the fifty miles to town before it would be too swollen to fix it. So I decided Dr. C. Shultz could set the nose herself. If it was going to get done, I was going to have to do it!

My nose was soft, bloody and slick. I rubbed some dirt on my fingers, got a hold of my marshmallow nose and quickly pulled and shoved it somewhere in the middle of my face, blood going everywhere. Then I laid down on a big flat rock to help slow the blood down and to get it to clot. Good thing a car didn't come by, or they would have thought someone had slit my throat and killed me, as much blood as there was.

The bleeding finally stopped, so when Bev came back with Skipper I got back on him. We had cows to chase! We rode for five hours running cattle, gathering and driving them up the ridge. My eyes were swelling shut and getting black, my nose was getting bigger all the time and hurt like you wouldn't believe. Skipper was constantly wanting to buck. I had my hands full that day.

I rode Skipper the next day to finish working the cattle. On the third day I went to the valley for two doctor's appointments and to pick up one of my old college friends that I hadn't seen for twenty years.

I went to the orthopedist, Dr. Baranco, to get my knee drained and injected. He looked at my nose and said, "I believe you'll be back in here to have nose surgery when the swelling goes down." I told him I thought Dr. Shultz had done a pretty good job.

When I went to get an allergy shot from my family doctor, he just stood there looking at me, grinning from ear to ear. He agreed that I would probably need nose surgery later.

I never did have nose surgery. My bifocals sit down on that part of the ridge of my nose, and it doesn't feel too good in cold weather, and sometimes I have trouble breathing, but Dr. Shultz did a pretty good job, I thought.

One August morning Joy Weaver came up, ate hot cakes with me and then helped me kick out a little salt here and there. Bev had to get started with school and in-service, and we needed to check the cattle and the salt in Green Field Flats before I left the following week. Joy and I loaded the horses and went up Pole Creek to look for cattle. We went to Lost Bull Creek, turned around and came back, unloaded salt at the big culvert at Pole Creek and then started up the canyon.

I was riding Skipper. I had forgotten to put my draw rein on him when I started, but he was doing pretty well. When we came down the mountain later, we rode to the plateau and my saddle slipped a little. I started straightening it, putting my weight gently on the other side. Skipper spooked.

I was off balance from trying to straighten the saddle and lost a stirrup. The next thing I knew I was on the ground with the wind knocked out of me. I hurt so bad I just lay there, curled up around a big rock. I had hit the only big rock in that whole meadow

It felt like there were several ribs gone. This was not the first time I'd had ribs broken, and I knew I had done it again.

Joy ran down Skipper, and I got up on one knee with much gritting of teeth, and tried to get in the saddle. I hung onto the stirrup and started pulling myself up but collapsed in utter agony.

"I cannot get on," I told her.

We were a long way out, an hour's ride to the truck and another hour's drive to the corrals. I had to get on.

Finally, I told Joy, "If I get up, grab me by the seat of the pants and throw me on no matter what I say."

Joy is slim built at about five foot ten inches, and I am a five-foot six-inch chunk weighing twice what she does.

Somehow she got me on Skipper. Later she told me, "I knew I had to get you on that horse, 'cause it had been a long time since I had been up in that country. I would have had to had taken all my clothes off and left pieces tied to the bush so I could tell somebody what to follow to come back to find you! So I knew I had to get you up there!"

The next day was my birthday. I was a mighty sore forty-two-year-old! I felt like I had sunk my floating ribs, and was sore, sore, sore from the scapula to the pelvis on the left side.

Still by myself, two days later the horses needed switched around to get rid of some of them before I left for school. Somehow I led Big Buck to the loading dock, straddled his bare back and rode him up the road a half mile. I thought my whole side would cut loose and come out, it was so sore.

Big Buck is rough riding, even when walking. I rode him through a gate to turn him loose for the rest of the fall. I thought I would try getting off a sixteen-hand horse gently. No such thing! Man, I hurt.

When I went to school three days later, I went to the doctor in case something was drastically wrong with me. I knew there wasn't anything he could do for broken ribs. The doctor I saw was not my regular family doctor and thought I was pulling his leg. I told him I didn't care what he thought, but just to give me some pain pills because we still had a lot of fall work to do on the ranch. When he looked at the x-rays, he really did think I was crazy! I had three or four broken ribs that time.

About three years later I traded some rawhide lariats for a desert-raised horse I named "Rawhide." I wasn't surprised he was spooky in the timber. I left him in the pasture for almost a month before I even tried to ride him.

It was a real experience riding him. Bev and I were driving cattle toward Pole Creek, and as we got into Woodard Camp, an old bull took off. That bull had been hard to collect, and I wasn't going to let him get away! Bev went on with the cows up the road and around the corner somehow without losing any. She's a good cowboy.

I turned the bull once right on the edge of the campgrounds. Luckily nobody was camping there that day. That bull turned to make a "dido," so to speak, through me *and* the horse, then ran toward the creek. I forgot for a moment that Rawhide was a desert horse and turned him to follow the bull.

There was a three-foot dropoff to a pool about three feet deep. The bull jumped over it all and into the brush on the other side. If I had been on Skipper, he would have jumped it, and we would have just kept going. Not Rawhide. About that time the bank gave way, and his back feet went down like they were going through a gopher hole. Then his feet were in the water and he started bucking like he was loco.

I lost my bad leg out of the stirrup and before I knew it, I was on the rocks by the water. Rawhide calmed down and started grazing, dragging the reins. When I didn't show up, Bev came looking, and when she saw Rawhide grazing in the meadow, her heart dropped. She knew I was hurt or worse. The dogs found me lying there and started licking my face.

What a situation we were in! Four miles from home, thirty pair of cattle gathered up, and I knew I had broken ribs and needed to get *home*. There was no other way but on my horse. Bev helped me up and wanted to ride home with me. I said, "Nothin' doin'." She wanted to ride home and get the pickup and come get me.

I said, "Nothin' doin'. I'll be so stiff by the time you get here that I won't be able to do anything, and we'll lose all those cows in the campground."

I told her she had to take those cows east up to Pole Creek no matter what, and I would start home. She wanted to know how I would get through the cattleguard and the gate, which was half a mile from the corral. I told her surely there would be some tourists come by. It seems like tourists were always around and in the way when we were driving cattle on the road.

I started out, gripping the saddle horn I hurt so bad. Rawhide seemed to know he had pulled a good one and that he better settle down. I thought we would never get home. We walked up one hill and down the other and around the corner. We met one pickup coming up the road and none coming down. That's all. By the time I had come the four miles to my upper cattle-guard, there was not a soul in sight.

I waited as long as I could for someone to help me get through. The horse was dancing and prancing, trying to rear. It was a killer doing it, but I finally let myself off the horse with my busted ribs, dragged open the steel gate, and led him through. I knew I could not hold him back, he was so excited to be close to home.

I put Rawhide's reins up over the saddle horn and said, "Have at it."

Off he went with all my good gear on, a mile to the next gate if he didn't stop at the corral. Then I started down the road. I had pulled my hip and leg muscles so bad I could not lift my leg. I had to drag it. My ribs felt like fire from a dynamite blast, and it was a hot day besides.

Just as I got to the corrals, here came a great big camper truck. I dragged myself out of its way, but it didn't stop. I'm sure the people in the truck couldn't help seeing I was hurt.

The horse was waiting for me, and somehow I managed to swing open a gate, drag the horse in and put him in a small corral so he couldn't roll with my saddle. I took the good bridle and reins off and just left him for Bev to take care of in a couple hours.

After taking some pain pills, I settled into the best rib-healing chair I've ever had—a yard sale special. And that's where I was when Bev came, white as a sheet.

Somehow Bev never seemed to get into any of these scrapes and accidents. She always rode a well-trained horse and picked the pieces up when I got in trouble. She could run a chainsaw, run a cow, pull porcupine quills, shoe a horse if she had to, and did more than her half of the work even when I wasn't laid up. She was a good partner.

One time I told Jack, our Forest Service supervisor, "If you wanna know what your cowboy's doin' on any of these allotments, sit back and look at the hat he's wearin'."

Jack looked at me and stroked his beard. He asked, "What do you mean?"

I said, "Well look at my hat."

Bev and I wore good felt Stetsons, and invariably mine would be busted out with holes punched in the crown. I said, "If your cowboy on some allotment's wearin' a straw hat, he's not workin.'"

"How come?"

"Well, Bev found that out the first year we worked. It was hot. It was that drought year, and she wore a straw hat when we went up to cut some trail out.

"Comin' home we took a shortcut down through some timber and brush with no trail, and she tore the whole crown out of that good straw hat. You cannot ride in the brush and dig these cattle out of the brush and keep your hat in one piece if it's a straw hat. After two years, I've had even the crown ripped out of every felt hat I have bought, I don't care how expensive it is."

He looked over at Bev and said, "How come hers isn't out?"

Bev said, "Carol rides a bigger horse and she's bigger than I am. She makes a bigger hole when she goes through the brush." She was right.

CHAPTER 11

FENCES, TRAILS AND CATTLE DRIVES

FENCES WERE IMPORTANT in controlling the cattle—where they grazed, how much and in whose allotment. We maintained several miles of fences in the timber in our allotment.

When fences needed to come down, the Forest Service was tickled to death to give Bev and me the job of taking them out. They would typically forget, however, to tell us exactly when they were going to close the logging road to the old fence.

One time we went back up to tear the fence down the week after we were told about it, and there was a huge dam of dirt lying ahead in the road. We scratched our heads, walked up the fence and looked around. I said, "I got it. I know how we're going to do this.

We went back to the house and got ready for the fence expedition. The next day was wonderfully cool, and we went back and started pulling out fence posts, rolling up wire and stacking it in strategic places. We used a wheelbarrow and loaded it with fifteen cedar posts six and a half feet long each trip. We ran a light tow chain around both posts and the wheelbarrow and used a light chain binder to tighten it. Then we put a lariat around part of it and hoped for the best.

We went down through the timber and rocks on a cow trail for several hundred yards. The last fifty feet or so was so steep I could not control the wheelbarrow. The only alternative to unloading it and Bev and I throwing all those fence posts and rolls of barbed wire by hand, was to give that wheelbarrow a big shove and let her go! I tried to grab hold of the lariat rope to tip the outfit over before it went down over a steep cut-bank. It worked out well. We could haul those fence posts out quicker than with a packhorse.

The only fences on most of these allotments were only drift fences—dividing the allotments into two halves. There were a few fences between allotments where the lay of the land made it easy for the cows to mix. Any private land in or next to the U.S.F.S. had to be fenced if the rancher wanted to keep Association cows out of his private grass. It was completely up to the private rancher to put these fences in and to keep them up and in good shape each year.

Our allotment had an old test plot fenced—long ago deserted. The U.S.F.S. was trying to get rid of a lot of old forgotten fences. If anyone wanted the wire they had to take any and all posts, etc. out with it—no matter if the posts were rotted off.

Fixing the fence on top of the mountain was kind of fun. At about eight thousand feet elevation, we could look down into Cascade Lake and watch the little toy boats on the big reservoir. If you had a good pair of binoculars, you could see some of the fish jumping down there! It was almost straight down to the reservoir, maybe a mile from the bottom of the mountain.

Most of our trail clearing was done up on the mountain, but sometimes the brush was thick down on the creek bottom in the campgrounds and needed clearing. We could hardly get a horse through it. Before the camping season started, we would take a chainsaw and cut a few holes so we could get through and get the cattle out of there without running through too many campgrounds. It was a never-ending job keeping cattle out of the campgrounds, and cutting holes in the brush really helped.

The Forest Service had a policy of clearing some of the more popular trails every seven years, five if you were lucky. You can imagine how bad the trails got from all the lodgepole and fir that would blow down every year. So we had to clean them up or we couldn't get anywhere up there!

Twice when we had cleared the trail, the Forest Service crew came in well after they knew we would have it clear, because we had to have cattle up top by the first of August. They brought their horses and made a big show of it, trimmed a little hatknocker off here and there that we hadn't bothered with. They called that trail clearing, but we had already done the work.

The first year we were on the job two government men in a Forest Service pickup were in our area. We didn't know what they were doing. One day we got a chance to visit with them, and found out they were clearing trails.

I said, "You don't have any chainsaws."

One of the guys answered, "No, the Forest Service said they didn't have any money for saws, so they just sent us pruners and some hand saws."

He told me they had come over Wilson Mountain, an area with fir trees three to five feet through at the butt.

"How did you manage that?" I asked.

"We didn't. But when I went home and told them what it was like, they agreed they'd find us some chainsaws."

"When you get that cleared out and don't know where else to go, I've got some more government trails you can clear."

One day they actually stopped and asked about trails to clear, and I said, "Meet me at the camp and I'll show you where to go."

I marked on their maps some trails that the government hadn't marked for them to clear but that hadn't been cleared for years. Those trails were cleared that year, thanks to them!

Another day they told us, "You don't want to believe all the trail markings comin' out of Green Field Flats!" That is at eight thousand feet elevation. "We got lost and went northwest. We should've been going southwest."

I said, "Did you mark it?"

"Yeah."

"Did you go back and just skin the tree and get rid of the dot and the dash markers?"

"No, we were really lost!"

Bev and I went up there later and no wonder they got lost. It was rough out there! It was a good cow trail, but it just went into the Poison Creek Basin, and then on out over the top. There are huge fissures where lava flowed up through cracks in the ground. A person couldn't walk across it, let alone get a horse across it. If I hadn't had a good idea where I was, I would have been lost out there, too.

Getting people to help us clear trail was sometimes entertaining. One of the most memorable times was Sunday, July 7, 1985. Gary Campbell, head of the racing commission for the state of Idaho, and one of his commissioners, Russ Westerburg, had been bugging us to take them to the top of the mountain. We were working cattle with some of their race horses, and the men had been told how beautiful it was up there, so finally I told them to set a date, and we would go. Bev was out for supplies that day.

The day came. While those two big men got their long-legged race horses out of the corral, I casually walked across the road to another corral and got Toby and Molly, our two little mules. I think Toby could have walked under the belly of Campbell's horse. I could see consternation and disappointment on their faces, but they were gentlemen and didn't say a thing.

I handed Campbell a steel fence stretcher. "What's this for?" he asked.

"We're gonna stretch some fence," I answered.

"Where at?"

I told him, and I gave the other guy two chainsaws and told him to put them in the overhang of the truck.

"What are these for?" he asked.

"You're probably gonna have to cut some trees out to get to where you're going!" I wasn't going up that mountain trail with two men without clearing trail along the way!

We loaded the animals and the things we would need, drove up to the helioKrissport, and started getting ready for our ride. I could see those men talking to themselves, kind of disappointed, on those great big long-legged racehorses. I got on Toby, and Molly pulled just great. She never jerked on the rope or anything, and we had the saws and everything on her.

I headed up the trail and never looked back. I was so stiff it was hard for me to look back anyway, and I figured two big grown men on those racehorses ought to be able to outrun me!

When we got to the first trees that needed cleared out, I looked back to see if they were all right; they were quite a ways back. When they caught up with me, their horses were sweating and huffing and puffing, worn out! They offered to do the cutting, so I let them.

On we went up the trail, cutting trees as we went. Suddenly through the timber, I heard, "Hold up, Carol! Hold up! My horse is in the creek!" And there they were, out in the middle of the creek, their horses heaving and sweaty, and about done in. My two little old mules, even fully loaded, worked circles around those two race horses.

After we got back, we had a bite to eat, and Campbell started talking. "You know, I never did think much of mules," he said. "When I saw you go over there this morning and bring those two little suckers back, Westerburg and I both thought we would never get to the top with those two little devils. We were sure we'd end up packin' 'em, and Carol, too, or she'd end up walking. I apologize. Now I have all the respect in the world for those two little mules."

Seven years later Doc Hyde told me, "Campbell's still talking about those two little mules and how tough they were and how they about literally killed those two racehorses. Don't undersell your two little mules!"

For several years snow was still on the upper part of the canyon at Squaw Creek during trail clearing and fencing time. Sometimes we had to walk over big snow drifts to get up the canyon or skirt out into an elk meadow. Then there would be trees down under the snow that we couldn't cut out!

One year we were on top in Green Field Flats at about 7500 feet putting up fence. It was July. There were two snow-drifts on the south end that were four feet deep, almost to the top of the post. We got the fence up because I was determined I was not going to come back later and fight the swamps I knew we would find then on the south end. I shoveled the snow out around that corner and out about ten feet, and we got the fence put up with snowdrifts six to eight feet deep nearby!

It was summer, and the grass out in the open was nice and green, about six to eight inches high. A few old cows that had found their way up there on their own were eating grass next to the snowbank.

The nice part of working near the snowbanks was that we could eat snow while doing the hot job of chainsawing. This made our job much nicer. We could sit and enjoy our lunch and a candy bar, eat some snow and put a little under our hats to keep us cool while we worked.

One of our main jobs was to drive the cattle from one area of the allotment to another so they could get the feed they needed.

There were always cattle that would get away from us, and we would have to go up and gather those "renegades" at some time or another. We couldn't always find them, but at least we had to look.

We moved some of them at night for the best luck, because they hardly knew where they were and would stay together better out on the range. It would take three of us to do the job, so we would often wait until someone wanted to ride along before we would take on this task. We would all three round up the renegades and ride up the road several miles. When we got by most of the easy places for the renegades to peel off, Bev would ride back home and get the truck. By the time she caught up with us it was dark, and we were in deep timber, but this way we could load up at the end of a midnight cow drive and ride home!

In the pitch dark some of those old, black renegades were hard to keep track of. We could ride right by them and never know it in all that brush and timber. But the dogs usually would bring them along.

It would be so dark we couldn't see the edge of the road, and in places it was a mighty long ways down to the creek. If we or a cow got too close, often the only clue was the sound of a rock rolling downhill.

We usually did this drive during the week so we wouldn't run into campers. There was a guy camping up there with his woman and kids, a camper, and a tent. We didn't know he was in the area until it was too late. We dropped thirty pairs of bawling cattle and four fighting bulls in their campground. We didn't stay to see what happened next.

The next day we went up there to make sure there were no strays. The lady came out and asked, "Was that you guys brought these cattle in last night?"

I nodded my head.

"Well, we were sound asleep and here come this bawlin' herd. Those bulls fought the rest of the night!"

She was not a happy camper, and I can't say I blame her. Probably the only worse thing would be if she had been there after I rolled a dead cow off the mountainside and hit her camp.

One day Bev and I were chasing cattle when, in their usual form, the cows split up. Bev went after one bunch, and I peeled down over the mountainside after more. Boy, were they wild! I could not get around them.

I thought, "Ah. You get down there and get in the swamp somewhere and tank up and then I can get around you." I was determined to catch those cattle!

We kept running down the mountainside, as steep as all get out. I was on my favorite Arab, Skipper, who was quite capable.

Every once in a while I would catch a glimpse of a cow or two. There was fresh manure strung out from a running cow, so I thought I could catch up.

After a while I noticed a difference in the tracks—they were a lot further apart! I had not only been chasing Herefords, but some elk also.

Poor old Skip. He was tired. I started him up and let him take his time. It got so steep he went to his knees like he was praying and just stood there. I got off, just like stepping off a stair, and let him catch his wind. Looking up the hill I thought, "That's too steep for this old lady, and if this horse is gonna make it without me, he can make it with me," and crawled back on him.

Several times cowboy friends of ours have come up to help but didn't know the mountain way of driving cattle.

Mike, a big fellow, came in the fall one year to take over so Bev and I could get back to teaching school.

It had snowed on top, and a lot of cows had come off the top of the mountain. As Bev and I went up the ridge and pushed out the cattle we found in the timber, they came down to the road where Mike was driving the growing herd. We had told him, "Mike, this is BB day: 'Beat their Butt Day.' You stay on their butt, and you keep this outfit bunched on that road or you're gonna lose 'em. This is our last day of workin' and they're all gonna be yours tomorrow!"

As a typical desert cowboy, he let them wander. We could see him doing it from way up on the ridge while we were driving more down. By the time we got caught up with him, all he had was a handful of cattle. He was pretty sheepish about it.

"I shoulda listened to you women. You knew best. I drove 'em like I would if I was out in the desert!"

I said, "Well, that's all right. Tomorrow you better be back up here a-pickin' 'em up and drivin' 'em, cause you got several days work ahead of you." I think he figured things out.

One of our favorite tricks was to take the horses in the truck about ten to twelve miles up the mountain, unload the horses, and start gathering cattle. We would gather cows for maybe an hour or two or three, whatever it took, in the hundreds and hundreds of acres of clearcuts.

Once they were on the road, we got them strung out and started down it. If we could get them past a certain area, they were much less likely to peel off on their own. One of us could handle the herd then, so Bev would ride back up several miles, load her horse in the truck and drive down the mountainside.

She could catch up with them in the truck, drive through the middle of the herd, and be down at the bottom of the mountain at Pole Creek waiting for them on her horse, ready to turn them into the pasture where they were to go.

One day we picked up some Ola C cattle with ours. Some of them had horns, and they were wild and wicked! I could not keep up with them even on my big horse. They just lined out and went. Before Bev got to them in the truck, they were running down the road. She got through them in the usual way. She's a pretty good truck driver.

I was trying to catch up with them when I came around a big corner and looked straight across a little canyon and could see them milling in the road. I thought, "What in the world? What have they got in that road they're trampin' to death?" I thought maybe they had gotten a cougar; cattle have been known to do that.

I spurred my horse around the bend and down the road in a hurry. When I got closer I realized they had two timber surveyors totally paralyzed by fear at the edge of the cut in the road.

The bulls were fighting, and the horned cattle were ripping into my cattle. In the middle of all this were these two timber surveyors, shaking like two sticks in a hurricane, white as a sheet.

When I got the cattle away from those timber surveyors, their knees were still shaking. The vibration probably wrecked all the cartilage in their knee joints. They couldn't even talk for a little bit.

"Are you guys hurt?" I asked. I didn't know who they were yet.

After a while they could speak. One of them remarked, "No, I guess we aren't."

I laughed and said, "You guys will need a lot of adrenaline to get on up the mountain!" And I went on. Not every day you can get one of those birds and get the upper hand. More often, they were in their pickups running our cattle for us, laughing at us. This time I had a good laugh.

The next day we went up to pick up more renegades. We parked the truck, rode up the road, and there were the two surveyors. They seemed leery about us being in the area and didn't want to talk to us.

I rode up and spoke to them, and they begrudgingly talked to me. I asked them what they were doing. They were in there surveying merchantable timber for future timber sales. (Though there were a lot of clearcuts in that area, there was big timber there, also.)

"We're going to be running cattle, and we're going to run 'em right up through there," I said, pointing at their map.

"Oh. That's where we were going to work today," one of them replied.

"If I were you I'd work somewhere else until noon, 'cause we're gonna be bringin' cattle up out of there. They're raunchy, the ones that's left are the devils, and there'll be some with horns."

I had warned them.

We dropped down into some little canyons and draws and eventually fished out cattle. We drove them up into the clearcuts and went back and dug out some more. Eventually we had about a hundred pair of the raunchiest cattle strung out in front of us.

I broke out of the timber with some cattle that were coming at a pretty good lick due to having dogs at their heels. I looked back, and there were the two timber surveyors! They were supposed to be doing live timber survey, but there they were in the middle of the biggest clearcut around, sitting up on top of the highest stump they could find, hanging on for dear life. Some of my cattle broke off and came up around them.

We never saw them after that. I think they saw our red truck coming and headed for the tallest tree.

CHAPTER 12

DEAD COWS

ONE OF OUR JOBS WAS TO LOOK for dead cattle. We needed to get their ear tag, check the brand, look for bullet holes, and take a picture so we can give the information to the owners. We also needed to know the cause of death when we found our animals dead. In the evenings we would drive slowly, use our noses, and search. The smell always came downhill on the evening breezes, so we would look uphill for the dead critter we were smelling. The opposite was true in the mornings, and we would look downhill—below us. That method helped us find quite a few dead cows!

Poison Creek was well named because of the larkspur. Cattle died in that stuff. A vet told me that when cattle get into larkspur, they quickly get addicted to it and will look for it even when there is other feed. Larkspur grows on lush creek bottoms and wet areas. Oldtimers have told me that a cow has to eat the roots to die. The botany book says the plant is most volatile at the bud stage, about when the cattle come by on their way to high pasture. If they pulled it up by the roots to get the poison, the plant would die out. We never did see any sign of root disturbance.

Larkspur dried naturally on the stem is not a problem for cows. If a cow has been eating fresh larkspur plants for very long, it is better just to leave her there; if you drive her, she'll will die. Interestingly, when a cow died in that stuff and started smelling bad, the rest of the cattle cleared out and left on their own, even before bear or vultures could find the carcass!

One time I tried doing what the oldtimers always said was the cure when a cow's sick from eating the larkspur. We were hauling salt on our horses when a cow stepped out of the timber. Her head was bobbing up and down like she was rubbing on a corral fence, and I thought, "That's odd." As I got closer I could see she was having trouble breathing. Then I knew she had gotten into larkspur.

I jumped off my horse, gave Bev my pack horse, split the underside of the cow's tail next to the body, curled her upper lip back and split that next to her gum. She was oozing what looked like cans of strawberry jam, thick and dark. There was no oxygen in it! Needless to say, she died shortly thereafter, and my "cure" didn't work.

One day we were taking a shortcut through the ranch on our way to work some cattle in the allotment. When we got to the creek we found a heifer lying dead in the middle of the water. She was big and had been trying to calve; we could see the calf's nose out. We had to ride on and finish our work, but when we came back, we wanted to get her out! That was all we needed, a dead cow in the creek. I have drunk out of creeks and then made the mistake of walking upstream and finding a dead cow in the water! Not healthy.

I threw a rope on her to get her up to the edge of the creek. I thought the current would help a little. I was riding Big Buck who weighed sixteen hundred pounds, but we could not budge that cow, she was so big. Buck pulled so hard his belly was almost touching the ground trying to jerk that cow, and she just wouldn't budge!

We had to go home, put the horses away, and come back with Bev's three-quarter-ton pickup. I waded into the creek with a chain and put it around the cow's head. The pickup groaned a little and spun in the loose dirt and rock, but we got her out.

Another time we were up Pole Creek and walked around the corner where we usually found dead cattle. We were afoot, late in the evening. The vultures had been eating all day and were so full they could hardly take off. When they did take off, they shot out so much excretion, it seemed like literally gallons of fluid dead cow. It was smelly. Now dead, rotten cow smells, but when you put it through a vulture and end up with second-hand dead cow being squirted at your head—courtesy of a departing bird—you have just discovered a new dimension of the term "nasty."

Luckily, I was looking up as one bird went over my head. I could see it was going to bomb us. I yelled, and everybody got out of the way. We about got plastered with that putrid stuff! We had to learn to look and dodge.

A fellow told me once how to skin a dead cow so I could use its hide for rawhide, and I was waiting for a chance to try it out. When a tourist came by one day and said, "You got a sick cow up such and such a place," I took off to see what was the matter even though I was alone. I stuck a knife in the pickup but didn't bother to see how sharp the blade was.

I found her, and she was deader than a doornail. I thought, "This is the time to pull the hide off." The ground was pretty flat, so I drove up closer with my little two-wheel Datsun pickup. I did what Frank told me. I took the knife and made an incision over the root of the tail and down the other side and up her belly, hooked the pickup on her and rolled that old sister over. I was in the process of making the backside cut when a pickup came down the road.

They were loggers, and I recognized them. They went by and they could see my pickup parked off in the bushes there, and it looked like I was butchering a cow. They got down the road a hundred yards, and started backing up.

I thought, "I bet they think I'm rustlin' somebody's cow. I wonder what they're gonna do—shoot first and ask questions later or what."

I stood up and looked. They pulled back, and then they recognized me. They were interested in what I was doing, so they came over to watch. They did not think I could pull the hide off that cow! I put a chain around the old cow's head and fastened it to the butt of a little Christmas tree. I fastened a chain around the cartilage in the ear butts I had cut loose and peeled back and hooked it onto the back of the pickup. I told the kid who was the catskinner, "You stand off to one side and watch now, and make sure I don't wreck something."

He shook his head. "It ain't gonna work."

I started easing the pickup forward, and the kid could see that it was working. He started jumping up and down like he was on a trampoline and yelling, "Give her hell, Carol! Give her hell, Carol!"

The cow's hide came off as neat as you take a sweatshirt off over your own head. Now there were two loggers convinced that this method worked. Eventually I made a rawhide lariat out of that skin.

Probably my favorite dead cow story happened when we were salting on Wilson Mountain. We were coming back home on one of the older logging roads. Right there on the edge of the road was a black cow, big as a fifty-gallon barrel, bloated, with legs sticking out like crutches. Its white face was black with flies. I said to Bev, "Here's my chance." I love to roll rocks or whatever down the mountain, and I could see instant possibilities here! I told Bev, "Here is my chance—grab a hold of those legs!"

Bev helped me, and we rolled that thing down a hill as steep as a cow's face. Over it went about three turns, then hit a little batch of Christmas trees. The little trees bent over, and on went the carcass to a big old fir tree. By the time the carcass hit that big fir it had really picked up speed. It split in half, and we had blood, guts, gore and smell going everywhere. Some of it kept going downhill, landing toward the camps. This was just before Fourth of July, and it stunk to high heaven. It really was ripe.

The next day we went back there to check on some things, and as we came through the camp someone stopped me and asked, "Cowboy, you got a dead cow around here?"

I said, "Darned if I know. Why?"

"Well it stinks." It was hot that day and it really did stink, but I didn't let on I could smell anything!

I told him, "Aw, it's probably your tenny runners you've got on. You need to get in the creek and wash 'em up!" We just drove on, grinning to ourselves.

One day we had spent all day driving cattle and checking the salt grounds and were heading home. We got partway back down to Poison Basin where we had seen a dead cow in the morning, and there sat a young two-year-old cinnamon bear. He sat downhill from that cow just like he was at a dinner table with both paws on her belly, his head buried in her side. We sat on our horses for a while and watched him enjoy his meal.

Another time we saw three black bears eating on a carcass.

The alder thicket was so dense I knew I wouldn't be able to get where I was going on my horse without Bev guiding me. "You stay up here and guide me, and then tell my insurance how I died!" I said, laughing.

I had to run the bears off, and they didn't want to go! I yelled and threw sticks at them. I did not want to get off my horse. Even at sixteen hundred pounds, Buck was no match for those three big bears if they had decided to gang up on him. I finally made believers out of them when I swung the rope against the alders.

They got off the cow and hid in the alders, but I could hear them snapping their teeth like Spanish castanets. The cow had been shot. The bears started back in my direction before I was through, so I yelled and threw things at them again. They weren't interested in leaving!

When I could see one of them and could hear the other two popping their teeth and going "woof, woof, woof!" I decided that was just a little too close. Some biologists will tell you that that's when they are ready to look at you for supper.

Afterwards I told Bev, "If they'd-a-come after me, crippled up as I was—batwing chaps and all, spurs caught in those bloody alder tangles—I'll bet I coulda been on top of that buckskin horse and never hit a stirrup." I was at their kitchen table!

One evening in July, 1979, I went up to Buck Mountain checking cows. Bev had gone for some supplies, and as I was coming home with my horse in the back of the truck, a sheriff's deputy stopped me.

"I got a call from a bear hunter that there was a cow butchered up here. Do you know anything about it?" he asked me.

"No. I haven't run across it."

He said it was "up here on Buck Mountain somewhere," giving the general description. "Will you go with me?" He had his wife with him, and it was early evening. I turned around and drove back up with them. He left his wife in the car to run the radio. He put his radio on, put his gun on, checked his ammunition belt, and checked the ammunition in the gun. I thought, "Gee willickers, here I am with nothing but a jackknife in my pocket, and he is armed to the teeth." I decided maybe I better stick with him. Maybe he knew more than he'd told me!

We walked around for probably thirty minutes, and it was getting darker. Finally he said, "Carol, you go this way, and I'll go over here and let's see what we can find."

I thought, "Yeah, you with all your ammo and the guns, and I don't have a thing." We hiked around and didn't find anything.

Finally it dawned on me what he had probably been told. About a quarter of a mile from there, further out on the mountain, there was a bear-baiting station. At that time anyone could haul anything in here they pleased to bait for bears. The bear hunters would bring up a flatbed trailer full of dead cows from the gut wagon. Who knows what they had died of or what bugs they were bringing in. They can't do that any more, thank goodness, in part due to our complaining.

I said, "I came through there a couple days ago, and there was a big Hereford bull head lying there in that area. I bet that's what it was."

So we hotfooted it over there, and it fit the description he had been given. If he had told me that to start with, I could have told him exactly what it was without having to go look. We did appreciate the fact that the law was interested enough to send a man thirty-five miles to look around.

CHAPTER 13

BULL CHASING

CHASING BULLS CAN BE EXCITING! You can expect them to not cooperate, and chasing them makes an otherwise boring day into something worth writing about. So here are a few tales.

One day I was chasing a bull on Ace, my cutting horse, a chunky Appy. We got that bull down to cow camp and were trying to get him across the creek when he led me into the brush. There he waited, then suddenly spun around and hit Ace right in the front shoulder. Ace and I were both on the ground, my leg caught under Ace on one side. We were in a pile of thorn brush, and he couldn't get up, and if he couldn't get up, I sure couldn't get out of the mess!

That bull started back in on us again. The brush was so thick that he hesitated a second, and I sicced the dogs on him in desperation. Those two dogs and Jiggs chewed the living daylights out of that bull. That's the only thing that saved me. We did get him in the corral.

The next morning we backed up a rig to the corral to haul him away. He could see the handwriting on the wall. He ran over to the fence, higher than my head, and reared up on his hind legs. He caught his front feet on top and walked on up with his hind feet stepping on those two-by-eight boards like they were a ladder. He teeter-tottered on his belly on top, pushed himself one more big "umph!" and over he went. I couldn't believe my eyes! He was a BIG hereford bull. Just climbed up like we had given him a ladder.

One of the funniest bull-chasing days of my life happened with a couple of good desert cowboy friends of mine. I will never forget that day! A desert cowboy's work just isn't the same as mountain cowboying, they finally learned.

Our good friend Bivens sold his cattle to Phil Solen. Solen brought in some high-priced bulls that I thought were a total waste of money. I told him so. They were too lazy to do their job. He always said he wanted his bulls off the mountain the first of August.

What a joke. Did you ever try to find eight bulls in twenty-six thousand acres of timber and brush? Obviously he hadn't, and he had no idea of what it was going to be like. He did agree to send a couple of men to help gather them.

Bev and I had a truckload of bulls gathered off the upper creek and mountain by late July. They were scattered from the campgrounds where several had been all summer by themselves—clear down the creek into the ranch, and two were down around the cow camp.

Solen sent his cow boss Vern and head cowboy Butch. Butch was the one that was going to do the dirty work since Vern was the boss. Vern wasn't going to do any more dirty work than he had to! (He was, by his own admission, a heavy equipment operator who had decided to get into cattle.)

They came in a big double-dual truck and backed up to the chute. We were talking about one particular bull I knew would give us trouble when Vern said, "Ah, we'll get him." The bull was in on my ranch.

I laughed and said, "Yeah, I've heard that before from your men."

"Ah," Vern says, "He can't be that hard to get. You've got all the brush cleared off of those meadows."

I rode Skipper, green broke and not wanting to look for a bull in August any more than I did. We rode down through the green gate and onto the meadows along the creek. The bull was under a tree where he always was, chewing his cud. He got up and stretched, giving us the impression that this was a Sunday School stroll.

Vern said, "He'll be chicken soup to get in that truck. That'll be nothin'."

Laughing, I said, "Hold on to your hat, boys." Vern went one way and Butch the other, and I got back where I knew that bull would head making his escape. As soon as that bull realized they were after him, he started to do his thing. He beelined it straight up the hillside to the gate, but before Butch could get there to open the gate, the old bull turned and bolted through the timber.

Butch and Vern were beginning to realize that this bull was not the little black angel they thought he was. When we did get him cornered and tried to push him back up the road to the gate, he bolted right through the two men and their horses and headed for the creek.

Butch started across the creek. I swear, a thorn bush reached out and grabbed his new Stetson. The hat dropped into the creek above his horse and floated down the water. His horse stepped on it with his hind foot, putting it two feet down into the bottom of the creek. The horse just stood there. Butch was swearing a blue streak!

Butch was wearing an expensive pair of new cowboy boots that came almost up over the calf of his leg. When he got off his horse into the creek, the water went clear up above his boot tops. He swore even more. He shoved his horse off of the hat, reached down into the water to his armpit, dragged out his wet Stetson, wrang the water out of it, and slapped it down on his head. When he jumped back on his horse, water was squishing and squooshing everywhere. Water was even running off his mustache. I could not keep a straight face.

Eventually, Butch and I got that bull rounded back up and around the meadow to the bridge. Then he made a run for it, and Vern couldn't stop him. It took the three of us another hour to get the bull back where we wanted him.

At loading time the guys somehow managed to get the three bulls we had already caught into the metal bed on the truck. Then those bulls got to working each other over in that truck, and I honest to goodness thought they were going to tip it over. It sounded like a first class war! People who were driving by came to a screeching halt to look. The truck sat on a side hill at the chute which made it look even worse.

Once the bulls were settled down, Vern asked, "Well, where's the next bulls?"

"Oh, there's two of them worse than this one."

"Aw, they can't be any worse." He did not believe me! "They'll be easy to get if they're up in the campgrounds." He was so sure.

I said, "Don't count your chickens before they're hatched."

We rode three miles up the road, spotted a monstrous old red bull, a big slow animal in the thick brush. I said, "You better leave him for now and pick him up when we come back."

They actually listened to me. We went on and found two other bulls in the campgrounds. It was not hard to control them with three of us, and as we were getting them to the road I said, "You desert cowboys better stay on their rears, because they're gonna give you the shaft."

"Once we get 'em on the road, they'll be easy. There ain't nothin' to this, Carol. You women—I dunno!"

I said, "You're soon gonna find out what us women's been tellin' you!"

We got the bulls on the road, and I said, "You better beat their butts and stay right on 'em, fellers."

Did they listen? Nah.

The next campground was about three hundred yards down the road, and Zap! Off they went! I felt like screaming! We rounded up one bull fairly easily, but the other one headed down to a thorn bush island in the creek. The stuff was growing so think on the ground that a person could not even crawl on hands and knees through it, let alone ride anything. That old bull just lowered his head and went for it. He evidently figured the deeper he got, the safer he was going to be.

The bull didn't reckon with Butch. Vern and I were up on the road, trying to corral the other bull, which we lost eventually, and we heard the worst noise down there, swearing and screaming and yelling. That old bull was a-bellering. Butch was picking up rocks big as his head and throwing them with a "Oooooo—Uh!"

After a while, Vern yelled down there, "You all right?"

"Yeah, I'm down here, but I need some help!"

Vern said to me, "Maybe we better ride down there."

When we were closer, we could hear Butch but could not find Butch's horse. He had tied up his horse and went on afoot after that bull. We rode back up the bank to the road in case the horse had come up, and after a while Butch had his horse and was on the creek in a little meadow with the bull! He must have given that bull a "high school diploma" about then, as we call "educating" the stock, because that bull was obediently moving down the creek and up on the road.

Again I reminded them, "Now fellers, stay on his butt. You're gonna lose 'im!"

Instead, those cowboys began to lay back again, had a smoke and watched that bull go down the road. They believed the bull had learned his lesson. Ha.

It wasn't long before we were within a hundred yards of my upper cattleguard and gate, I told him, "One of you better go hurry up and open that gate."

"Nah, he'll stand and wait. We've got him educated!"

That feisty bull knew what a bunch of high school dropouts he had driving him, and we lost him again, right at the cattleguards where it was a lot brushier than down on the creek where he had come from. Over the bank he went like a flash. Butch and I were right on his tail. It took two of us and a couple of good dogs, but we got him back up on the road and Vern had the gate open. Good thing.

By now he had gotten away how many times? I said "Now fellers, I don't want this guy in my pasture. You stay on his tail and get him through here!"

They had a smoke, which wastes a lot of time. We got down the road another eighth of a mile, and that fool bull bulldozed through my good stretched four-wire fence! I was mad!

There were alder thickets and wet spots where he was headed, and the old bull dove into the biggest alder thicket there was, probably a quarter of an acre. Once again Butch tied his horse up, and Butch and the bull stood there in the thicket and bellered back and forth at each other for probably ten minutes.

The leaves of that whole alder patch were bright red, and the more the two growled at each other in there, the more the alders shook. Butch chopped a two-inch diameter alder with a big machete-like knife he always packed and sharpened one end of it. He had a nice javelin about ten feet long, and could reach through the brush and prod that bull. He would heave it at him with a big "Uuumph!" We could hear it hit him. That old bull would let out a beller and a snort, and move a few feet.

The brush shook and wobbled, and that old bull began to work himself out of the middle of the swamp. He was bellering and blowing snot, looking for a fight. Butch staggered out after the bull, swearing and yelling. He was bloody from one end to the other, his shirt torn, his old wet hat down over his ears and eyes, his spurs dragging, and his boots still sloshing black water and swamp mud. What a sight!

He reared back (he was as strong as a mule) and threw his alder javelin at the bull. The javelin hit the bull on the inside of the hind quarter, almost making an "it" out of the bull right on the spot! I don't think Butch cared.

The bull's head and tail went straight up in the air, and he let out a beller you could have heard clear to Boise. Then he took off. He cleared a drift fence like it was a feather, went up on the road and through the open gate. We had no more hit the road ourselves when the bull made another bulldozer swipe through *another* four-wire fence. They thought I was mad before.

Butch and I went down into that mess and dug him out and got him back up on the road. I said, "Now fellers, does this make a believer out of you? That you better get on his blankety-blank rear end and stay there if you're gonna get him home?"

"Yes, ma'am. Yes, ma'am."

On we traveled. I stopped to talk to my forest service boss who had come along. It wasn't long before those two had let that confounded bull get off that road, and he ran down toward the creek and hit my fence again!

I did not want to face this mess the third time. But I finally decided that for the preservation of my fences I had better go down there and help them out.

I could hear them in the creek, and the noise was fierce! Vern and Butch were both swearing. Butch was off his horse, picking up rocks as big as his head, throwing them at that bull like bullets. The rocks hit the bull's horns with the sound of a .22. The bull shook his head, bellered, bawled and blew snot everywhere, then stood there, pawing the water and daring Butch to throw another one. When the bull saw me coming, he turned and started down the creek and into the brush.

I started down the creek after him. There was a fisherman I had told earlier in the day to get out of there. I yelled, "Watch out! There's a mad bull coming! Get out!"

All hell broke loose as Butch and the bull broke out of the brush. That fisherman made a hole in the brush big enough to put two bulls through. He was shaking like a leaf when I came by. I reminded him, "I told you this morning you better get out of here and stay out of here."

"But my fishin' hole was so good," he said.

"Well," I said, "Get out of here while you can still walk! We're not through yet."

All told, it took us an hour to find that bull and three hours to catch him! Once we got to the truck, Butch tried to put a divider up to keep these bulls somewhat separated.

He just about got himself killed again. The new bull started fighting with the old ones in the truck. When he saw

Butch afoot in there, he literally applied a horn under Butch's posterior and pushed him right out over the top of that truck like you would flick a fly! The sides of the truck must have been eight feet high plus the height of the truck itself, and the truck was sitting on the side of the hill, so Butch probably fell fifteen feet, landing more or less on his feet. He came up swearing, picked up a rock and threw it at the truck, and the bulls started fighting all over again.

Vern and Butch finally got the four bulls dumped in their home corral. Butch went to bed early that night, slept in late, kicked his wife out of bed and said, "Go feed them bulls while I sleep again." He was bushed.

It wasn't long before his wife came back again and said to him, "You know that one bull got a big rip on his hind leg, and he's lying down. I think he's dead."

Butch rolled over in the bed, picked up the phone and made a long distance phone call to the boss. "Phil, one of your thousands of dollars worth of bull is dead out in the corral," he said, and hung up.

Eventually Butch got up, ate a bite and went out to survey the damage. The bull was up on his feet! Limping pretty good, but alive. Butch went back into the house, made another long distance phone call and told the boss, "Hey, you know the bull I thought was dead? Well, too bad he ain't, but he's alive."

CHAPTER 14

JIGGS AND OTHER GOOD DOGS

OUR DOGS WERE GREAT HELP when we drove cattle. Running cattle on the mountain like we were, with timber and brush, big gullies and rocks, it takes two dogs to do the job, and sometimes we wished we had three good ones. We always tried to have two dogs with us.

Some dogs we borrowed for the summer and returned in the fall; we would have to find homes for the others. We couldn't have done our job without our dogs. They were great watchdogs, too, and we appreciated that.

The dog we had the longest was Jiggs. We got him the first year we were working for the Association, and we had to have him put to sleep fourteen years later. He lived a long and fruitful life, even as rough as his life was. He was a hard one to live with, and we had to keep him busy, but he was a good worker.

Jiggs, "The Enforcer," a big blue-heeler.

Jiggs was a big blue heeler with a short tail, wiry hair, and a head on him that made him look like he was part German Shepherd. He was a big dog, a natural heeler, loved to work, and smart as a whip. That dog could sit there, look at the cow, look at where I was wanting to go. I would just point and away he would go.

When Jiggs was only a few months old, before we got him, he got bit on the lip by a rattlesnake and packed a scar to his death. The bite almost killed him and cured him of ever wanting to mess with rattlesnakes again. It was easy to tell when there was one around if Jiggs was with us. If you got the best of Jiggs one day, you better watch out because he would even the score sometime down the road. My friend Bob Wolford, who kept Jiggs in Wilder over the winters, had that experience.

One day Jiggs wouldn't come out of his doghouse for Bob when it was time to clean up around there. Bob just tipped the dog-house over on its door and let him sit for about two hours. When he tipped it back up, the dog come out, snarled at him and went on his way. Bob laughed.

That same week Bob was carrying a big cardboard box by the dog house, and all of a sudden Jiggs grabbed him by the seat of the pants and gave him an awful good pinch. Bob said, laughing, "I knew he would get me one time or another."

Jiggs was kept on a twenty-foot chain a lot of the time when Bob was working. If a chicken came around, he was dead if he got within twenty feet of him. Bob said he always knew when Jiggs had killed a chicken because he would be repentant and friendly when Bob came home from work. Bob would find a fresh-dug hole, and there would be a chicken.

As a young dog Jiggs loved to come along behind and bug our horses. He would run his nose down around the horse's leg and spook it. One by one the horses got wise to him.

As he got older and we got other dogs, Jiggs would teach them how to run cattle and handle other tasks. When he was older still, he got the younger dogs started running up the trail, hill or road. The young dogs would take off and outrun him. Old Jiggs slowed down and let them do the work. He was no dummy! If an old cow had run off the edge of the trail, he would sit on the trail and look down over the edge, watching the young dogs in the brush trying to get the cow.

One day Ringo, another dog we had, was seriously cornered by a cow. The cow started pushing him right into the ground and would have killed him except for the foot-thick dust on the logging road. I yelled for Jiggs. What a dog! He went up one leg and down the other chewing on that cow until she got off Ringo.

Jiggs did a lot of things like that, and it was always fun to watch him work, figuring out what the next step was, where the next cow was, and "How am I gonna get that cow out of the bush?"

We could send Jiggs into a pile of brush, and if he needed help, he would start barking. Otherwise, either the cattle would come out or he would come out and look at me, as if to say, "Well here I am. What are you waitin' on?"

We never had to go through a brush pile if Jiggs had gone through it. And he taught several other dogs that same thing in his lifetime.

But he did have a few bad habits. There were times when we would be saddling up in the corral with Jiggs watching from under the tack shed. I think he was making plans. When we had the horse about half saddled, Jiggs would make a big swing through the corral, spook the horses, and we would lose the saddle. If the horse was a green horse or a bronc, it got wild. We were tempted at times to kill that dog.

Jiggs learned early on to come when he was called. As he got older, he taught the other dogs that when I had a certain tone of exasperation in my voice, they had better listen up. He would wade into the water after that dog if need be to teach him a lesson.

Jiggs and Shorty, another good dog of ours, loved chocolate. When we were fixing fence in the spring, he would beg for the candy bar we were eating. He would lick the paper and then start chewing on it.

Bev and lunch with two beggars, Shorty and Jiggs.

Another thing Jiggs liked to do was chew on the brush as we drove by in the pickup. He would stand in the back of the pickup, his feet up on the wheelwells or on the edge if we didn't have a stock rack on. He would lean out, looking intently, and make a grab. He didn't care whether it was thorn brush or pine trees, he would grab it and hang on until either it dragged him out or he broke it off. He left the back of the pickup looking like a magpie's nest hit by a hurricane.

One time we were going up the main road in our three-quarter ton pickup, moseying along looking for cattle. Jiggs was in the back of the pickup. A half mile up the road we needed to stop or slow down real slow for some reason, and here he came trotting, his tongue hanging out of his mouth. All we could figure out was that he would grab some brush and was so determined to get it that he let it drag him right out of the pickup.

Jiggs always wanted to be physically into whatever we were doing, his nose right there, inquisitive, and always in the way. On a hot day, he would walk in the shade of the horse. If there was any water or mud in a barrow pit, watering hole or just a dip, he would be in it, wallering. I miss Jiggs.

I had Jiggs in the front seat of the pickup when I picked Stubby up from Nadine, a teacher friend in Ontario, Oregon. The two pups were six and nine months old, big and overgrown.

Nadine had warned me to stay in the pickup if she wasn't home when I got there. For good reason. Stubby was long, lanky, yellow-gold in color, with big sharp teeth, and hated the world.

I got to their house just after noon and only Nadine's mother was there. "Oh, I can load that dog for you," she said.

"Fine. I'll drive out to the dog house, out in the barn yard." I had my three-quarter ton Chevy pickup with a stock rack on it, already two-thirds full. When I backed up, Stubby came unglued.

He was chained up, and I got out but there was no way I was going to help that poor old lady put anything in my pickup. She told me, "I'll take the dog and get him out of the way. But you're gonna have to get out of sight first. Go around the other side of the haystack."

So I walked out of sight. She took the dog and chained him up out of sight. I came back and helped her put the dog house in the pickup. When I went back out of sight, she got the dog into the pickup, in the dog house and started to nail a board on the front of the dog house door. He was having a fit.

She yelled for me to help her. I didn't know whether to come or not, because I knew if he got out of the dog house he would inhale me! We finished nailing boards on the front of the dog house, and Stubby was snarling and biting at the boards and trying to get at me something awful.

It was a hot day, but before I could go up to the ranch I needed to pick up some things at my home in Caldwell thirty-five miles away. I thought I would be nice to Stubby, so I got a little pan of water and stuck it in his dog house. He was so mad he wouldn't even drink. He wanted at me! I right quick loaded that pickup, closed the stock gates and took off for the ranch.

As I drove I wondered how I was going to get that hot dog out of there without him eating me, my "wooden leg" and everything else.

It was evening by the time I got to Bear Creek. I backed up by the woodshed and stopped. "Here's where I'll dump him," I thought. I got out, and then I remembered he had a twenty-foot chain on. "I can't even get in the woodshed to get any wood if I drop him here," I told myself.

I moved the pickup down the hill toward the footbridge and stepped it off. I decided I could make it running to the wood shed without him getting me if I put the dog and his house there.

I jerked the big doghouse out, dropped it on the ground and thought, "Now just how in thunder am I going to do this?" Stubby was coming unglued again. I got some gunny sacks and old blankets, took the shovel handle and shoved them in under the cracks around those boards to slow him down a little and then set out a pan of water.

I ripped one board off entirely, jerked the other one loose and took off running. Stubby scrambled out of the house, hit the end of his chain, jerked the house around and then acted like he didn't see anything.

We became the best of buddies in a few days since I was the only one to feed and water him. He didn't really have a choice! Stubby had a lot of blue heeler in him, and was a natural with cattle, never afraid to wade in and bite.

He was a dog nobody up there really liked, but they couldn't help but respect him. Folks figured out real fast if they came up our drive way when we weren't there, honked and saw Jiggs and Stubby, they either stayed in their rig or just drove on.

Even if Bev or I were there we had to watch Stubby. He would come around between the pickup and the brush, sneak under the pickup on the passenger side, and wait for the driver to put one boot down on the ground. He would grab that foot, not just goofing around, but playing for keeps!

We had a bed set up on the porch on high sawhorses, a nice place for cool breezes on hot afternoons. The dogs loved getting under that and waiting for some poor innocent person to sit down on the bed. Stubby taught Jiggs how to grab legs and feet dnagling from the bed. Stubby never did like people. He would as soon eat jeans as dog food.

Stubby learned to ride in the overhang of my three-quarter ton Chevy pickup. We would tie him in so he couldn't get down on the floor with the horses in the pickup. He would see a cow and get excited and jump over the front towards the hood of the pickup. There he would dangle, back feet a-scratching your windshield and clawing like mad and a-whining. You would have to stop and climb up there and untie him and push him back in. Once he did that three times the same day.

Jiggs and Stubby were pals and worked well together. Jiggs would catch a squirrel and not know what to do with it, and Stubby would come along and take one bite and kill the squirrel. Stubby wasn't fast enough to catch squirrels, but he sure helped Jiggs kill them!

Stubby and Jiggs both got into porcupine quills, and don't think it wasn't fun getting them out of buzz-saw Stubby! Thank goodness he learned fast and didn't get into them again.

Jiggs wasn't that lucky. The second time Jiggs got into porcupine quills, I thought I might have to take him to a vet. But good old emergency-room Doc Olson was here and helped me. Jiggs was just like a tiger! I put a stick in his mouth, a twitch on it, and sat on him in the middle of the tack shed while she extracted. What a job!

We were desperately needing a dog when we got Shorty. One day our ranching friend Janet Carlock said, "My brother Cliff's got a dog I think he'll loan you. In fact, I'll loan him, because I'm the one that has to take care of him! He's gone logging, and never sees him. Stop up there at the trailer on the big curve as you go back up to the highway, and take a look in the horse trailer and see if you're interested." Janet and Pat Carlock lived in the Ola Valley.

We looked. There was a little year-old blue heeler starving for affection. He made up with me right off. I told Bev, "There's a dog for us."

Bev was not convinced. He was small and didn't look like he could do a whole lot. Later we found out what people were saying about him.

"That Ola dog; he'll never amount to a hill of beans."

"He's worthless."

A neighbor lady who had a little trouble speaking English saw to it he had feed and water. She hated him! And I suppose he didn't like her any better because he was pretty sharp at perceiving what people think.

Once school got out that spring, Bev went to pick up Shorty. I was already done with school and had moved into the ranch house. Bev tied Shorty in the back of her pickup just as we would do with any dog that was learning to stay put in a pickup. He promptly jumped out and hung by the rope, twice. Bev had to tie him short enough to the spare tire so he wouldn't kill himself.

Shorty arrived in 1982. One day I was working behind the tack shed, fixing some things, and I heard a pickup come by and stop on the road. I was trying to keep an eye on Shorty, because he was kind of a traveller.

I recognized the white dog in the pickup. It belonged to Homer Nesbitt, but I didn't recognize the pickup. I went back to fixing the fence or whatever it was, and after a while, I realized Shorty wasn't anywhere around, and I about had heart failure. I was there by myself, and we did not own the dog yet.

I started down the road in the pickup, calling and whistling. No answer. The further I went, the more discouraged I got. I got two-thirds of the way to the fork of the road, about four and a half miles, picking up cans along the way to make the roadside look a little better. I stopped and got out to pick up a can, and here came Shorty.

He was wet and muddy. He had been shortcutting back up to the ranch. I don't think he knew how to get there because we hadn't had him that long. Was he glad to see me!

Shorty had one bad habit. If we would bend over to pick him up, he would turn over and squirt! He was an effective fire hydrant.

We didn't know what his original name was. I tried every name I could think of for that dog, and he didn't respond to anything. Finally, because of his very short stubby tail I called him Shorty. He turned around and picked his ears up and looked at me as if to say, "You've got it!"

Shorty had never run cattle. He learned. He would get up on a hillside with us above the timber and watch what Jiggs was doing. After a while, he came down to the trail where there was room to maneuver, looked at a cow and acted like he intended on going up and hitting the cow with his nose. Before the week was out, he was chewing and biting cow heels as well as the next one. Shorty wanted to work in the worst way.

He practiced at home. We always knew if we had a good heeler in a pup, because often before you knew it, they started bumping our bare heels with their noses. And then the next thing—they would be trying to heel the chickens at the corrals! Shorty was doing it all.

We worked Shorty two summers and returned him to Ola when school started each year. The first year I told Carlocks tongue in cheek, "Now remember: he's gotta have his own recliner and fireplace and a dish of popcorn every night if you're gonna keep him happy."

It broke our hearts to see him go back to Cliff's horse trailer again. He was fed and taken care of, but he had no companionship.

During spring vacation after his second summer with us, we took him on "visitation" for a week. They were glad to get rid of him. When I brought him back, Janet just says "Why don't you take that pup home with you? I'm tired of him. We don't use dogs." So we took him home.

Cliff was not happy with that decision, but he was away logging and didn't seem to care enough to do anything about it. Shorty went to live with Bev and her folks, and has been with one or the other of us ever since.

One day Cliff showed up drunk and wanted to take Shorty home. We weren't about to give him up, knowing he was getting much better care with us—and he was a good worker. Cliff insisted we give his dog back.

Things were getting pretty serious, when finally he said, "I'll tell you what. I'll call the dog, and if he comes to me, he's mine. If he goes to you, he's yours."

I could see there was no way out. I was going to have to take him up on it. As I said already, I didn't know what the dog's original name was, but we called him Shorty. The owner called, "Here Bandit. Here Bandit," and the dog came toward him. At the last minute he jumped up on me. I knelt down, my arms around him, tears in my eyes.

The guy said, "Well, I'll live up to my word. He's yours. I can see you're giving him a good home." He never came back. Shorty was a special dog, and I was happy to keep him.

Any dog likes rawhide, and Shorty was no exception. We had moved a little Forest Service building onto the property to use as a rawhide shack. I had been braiding a lariat, or *riata*, and Shorty was right there with me. I quit to rest, went to the house, and when I came back the door was open a little, and rawhide strings were strung through the snow and into the timber. The snow was about two feet deep yet, and we could see where he had bellied out in the snow.

I was just sick. I had the lariat about two-thirds done, and he had finished it up for me! The lariat ended up only about forty feet long when I got done, instead of fifty-five. Shorty completely ate up one string. To this day Shorty loves to lie down in my shop, either at the lower ranch or upper ranch, under the workbench in front of my feet, and wait for the goodies to drop down on him.

Many people thought Shorty was Jiggs' pup, but they were no relation at all. One was a big old blue and the other a little prancing blue. They worked well together.

Shorty loved to work with bulls. The bigger the better, because the harder they fell. On one cattle drive up a logging road, we picked up about five bulls. Bulls get tired and go toward the back of the bunch. Since the whip doesn't mean much to a lot of the bulls with their tough hide, we would sic the dog on them when they started lagging.

One bull learned to move up with the cows again when we just said "sic 'em." He knew who I was talking to! But one big Hereford wouldn't budge for anything except a dog. Shorty chewed on him for so many miles, that bull finally, out of desperation, starting bucking and literally walking on his front feet, bawling and bellering, trying to stay away from Shorty and his little teeth.The dog didn't weigh thirty-five pounds, and that bull was over a ton.

Best thing about Shorty was that he was a good companion. He let me know when the telephone rang at the lower ranch, or when somebody had arrived at the upper ranch. He was a good set of ears for me, since I'm rather hard of hearing.

Probably one of my favorite dogs was Snoopy, a border collie. Bill Stevens came up with three three-month-old pups and said I could have my pick. Snoopy looked like he needed a friend. He was a timid and lovable pup.

To train Snoopy, I put a rope on him and took him on short jaunts. One day toward the end of the summer I figured he was old enough to go to the top of the mountain on a rope while we packed salt.

I led Snoopy along. When he got tired about halfway up the mountain, I got off, tied him to a tree like you would tie a horse, and left him. That evening when I came back through there, he was glad to see me and stayed right with us.

He would be so tired after those first long trips that he would lie down at the cabin when we got back to Bear Creek, and wouldn't even get up to eat. We would place the food beside him, and he would lie there and eat and drink. He would not even get off his belly!

By the end of Snoopy's second year, he was working well. I was impressed. As a pup he once got under Big Buck. Buck stepped on Snoopy, not too seriously, but that pup thought he had been killed!

Bev got off, picked him up, handed him up to me on top of that big horse, and I hauled him home in my arms and on the saddle horn like a calf. He loved the attention.

One day Bev and I were hauling hay into the ranch with our truck and pickup loaded high. Bev took Jiggs and Snoopy on top of her load because it wasn't quite as high as mine was; if they fell it wouldn't be so far to land. I followed her to keep an eye on them.

Bev was quite a ways ahead of me when I came through Crane Creek. I came around a corner out in the middle of nowhere and saw a couple bales of hay, and some cows. I thought that was odd. But no dogs, so I kept going.

When I got to the top of Dodson Pass and passed the man-made stock ponds, I looked in my mirror, and here came two black, slimy critters after me. Were they my dogs? I stopped, they caught up with me, and they had both been in one of those stock ponds.

Snoopy and Jiggs were as black as the ace of spades, dripping wet with black slime. There was no way I could get those dogs to the top of my twelve-foot load. I had to clean them off a little with sagebrush and grass, and made room on my fairly new truck seat. The dogs were tickled as anything to ride inside, but what a horrible mess they made.

We got home, and Bev couldn't figure out why it took me so long. I said "Well, look at your load. You've got hay back on Crane Creek." Jiggs had apparently been barking at cattle or fooling around on top of the load and dislodged two bales. The dogs went off with them and for three miles they followed Bev!

We hauled our salt tubs (big inside-out tires) in the back of the pickup, and there always seemed to be a couple of empty ones. The dogs liked to curl up in those tires and ride. Snoopy soon discovered his favorite tub, and he really liked it.

One day I came back and couldn't find Snoopy, so I started down towards Weavers to see if I could find him. I figured he probably was dead. I stopped and called for him everywhere. When I got to Weavers, there he was, stretched out in the shade. Joy had fed and watered him. She knew whose dog he was, and she knew we would be along. She said, "Yeah, he's been here all day. Soakin' it up."

During Snoopy's third summer, Bev was gone to a physical education convention, and I had a bunch of cattle to move up Pole Creek and on toward Poison Creek. I had about fifty cows with their calves, too much for one guy to shove in that terrain. I thought about what I was going to do.

I told Snoopy to stay, went up in the middle of the herd and took half of them on up. When I got up to where I had planned to turn the cattle at right angles off the trail and up a draw, I knew I had to get ahead of the cattle. I looked back and there was Snoopy. He knew where I was going to turn them off the trail, and he helped drive them where it normally took two of us riders. He loved to herd.

That was his last season. Snoopy got run over on the road that fall and was killed.

Jack was a dog that belonged to Don Roberts, a foreman for Dave Bivens and got lost on the mountain. He warned us about Jack. He said, "He's mean. But "I'll be back in three days. If you can't handle him, don't worry about him." That mean dog was so tickled to see a human with some food that when he came to camp, he settled in and made himself at home. He was friendly. I guess any port in a storm'll do.

Bill Stevens brought Blue to us. Blue had long shaggy hair and glassy eyes like an Australian Shepherd and was supposed to be a good working dog. He wasn't.

Bill drove up in a fancy newly-painted blue Impala convertible with its top down. We were in the corrals working. Bill said to us, "Boy, I've got one for you!"

He went around and opened the trunk, and there was the most pathetic big blue dog I had ever seen. He had gotten terribly sick in that trunk and heaved his socks all over that redone, refurbished trunk and all over Bill's bedroll. He was still heaving when Bill took him out. That was our introduction.

We found out right away that the dog didn't even have sense enough to jump up in the back of a pickup; we had to help him. He wouldn't follow a horse even to come off the mountain!

One day we came off the mountain from salting all day, and when we got to the truck, he wasn't with us. I told Bev I was not going to ride back up that mountain to find him. If he came home, fine, and if he didn't, the coyotes could eat him. I knew we would be back the next day dumping more salt.

The next day we found him halfway up the mountain, waiting for us. He was glad to see us! He stayed with us a little better after that, but never was worth his salt. By the middle of the summer I called Bill and told him to come get his dog, or I was going to kill him. I was mad at Blue!

Chet was another first-class high school dropout dud. He was a red heeler and came from good bloodlines. Chet belonged to Joe Witty, agriculture teacher at Adrian High School. Chet had worked cattle a little for Joe, but then Chet got into chickens!

"If you can get him to work, bring him back. If you don't, I don't want to see him again." I was short of dogs, so I took him up on it.

That dog was dumber than a crutch or smarter than us, one or the other, I'm not sure which. He wouldn't follow our horses, so I finally threw a rope on him and forced him to come with me three or four mornings in a row. When we would get to cattle, the only reason he might chase a cow was because it was in the middle of his beeline straight back over the ridge to the house. And he was gone! He never did look at a cow.

We would ride home in the heat of the day, and there that dog would be, on the porch railing on the back of the old davenport—like a king on his throne, watching the butterflies and smelling the flowers, tickled as all get out to see us.

To make a long story short, I dry-gulched that loser. That fall when I went back to school, we had a freshman class that was really a corker and a half, and there were some kids in there that were pretty raunchy. The same kids gave Joe a bad time out in the shop class.

He told the kids one day, "If you don't straighten up for Ms. Shultz, you're asking for trouble. I sent her a dog this summer and she dry-gulched the thing. He never came home. She might do something like that to you guys if you don't wise up."

From that day on, I had very little trouble with that bunch of kids. They flew pretty straight. I couldn't figure out what made the difference for a week or two, until Joe told me the story.

A friend in Wilder brought a dog up to us and said, "I've always wanted a good stock dog and now I've got one. Go try him." He just called him "dog" because he hadn't had him very long.

He had a lot of border collie in him. He had a white neck and apron and a stripe on his butt about two inches wide from one flank up over the root of his tail and down to his other flank. So I called him Ringo.

Ringo was a lovable dog and worked pretty well for a dog with no experience. He was a nose-getter. If there were two other dogs working and had the heels tied up on a cow and the old cow turned, he would jump in, grab her by the nose and hold on for dear life. The cattle soon learned when Ringo was around that their noses were in peril if they turned and tried to take a horse or a dog!

Ringo was loyal but would work for just about anybody. He loved to work and loved riding in the truck. Even after he went to live with the Weavers, whenever I visited them in my stock truck, he just went crazy, wanted in that truck and wanted to go.

Once we were fixing fence up around Gill Springs before some of those roads got put in there. Ringo, Jiggs and Shorty had come with us. We got almost down to the ranch before we realized that Ringo wasn't with us. We were so tired I said, "I'm not going back. He can come home. He's been here before."

We had company, and we were sitting there cool and comfortable eating barbecue steak in the yard. I looked down at the road, and saw something that looked like an old black bear waddling around the corner. Ringo had sore feet, and his tongue was hanging down to his toes. That little stub tail he had was a-wagging a hundred miles an hour, he was so glad to get home. He stayed with us after that.

One year early in July we were up trying to dig cattle out of campgrounds, and Ringo and Shorty were two young dogs. They were full of it and they liked to work, and Jiggs sat back and let them work.

We were pushing cattle across the creek. I was on Dutch, and Mary Awohi was on a race horse we called "Freeway" because of how fast he could go if he wanted to. But he also could be very stubborn and then we called him "Dipstick." That day "Dipstick" fit him better. He wouldn't go across the creek. We got to yelling at the cattle we had been chasing in the brush and the dogs were excited. When Mary couldn't get Dipstick across the creek, the next thing I knew, Ringo had heeled him. That's all that horse and Mary needed. I couldn't get Ringo off. And Shorty was trying to heel him, too. I got off, swung my big heavy quirt and landed one on Ringo. He weighed sixty pounds. He turned around and looked at me as if to say, "Is that right?"

He went right back and heeled that horse again because Mary was still trying to get him across the creek. I gave him two good licks. Shorty was in on the foray, too, but I couldn't get my hands on him.

Shorty was still looking at the heels. I managed to catch up with him, got off my horse and gave him a good quirt. I got back on, and they tried to take the heels of both our horses. I got off again and gave them another dose of quirt. That time Shorty caught it on his tail. He didn't like that one bit. He headed for the creek, jumped in, swam out where I couldn't get at him and was laughing all the way.

I threw a clod at him, and that made him mad. Then we couldn't get either of the dogs onto the cows. They wouldn't chase a cow. And when we finally got them to chase a cow, we couldn't get them off. We had a four-ring circus there for a while. Dipstick wouldn't work, we had cattle everywhere, and the camp-grounds were full.

Somebody said we looked like an overfilled popcorn kettle down there with the cows and the horses and the dogs all going every which way.

CHAPTER 15

FEED AND WATER TO GO AROUND

BEV AND I WERE CAREFUL to watch for overgrazing. That's the first step to be sure of having enough feed for the cattle. Unfortunately, there have been many sheepherders and cowboys who didn't think about it, and the people after them have paid for their neglect by not having enough feed, and by having to reseed. And reseed we did.

The biggest reseeding job I know of up here happened some time after the Forest Service came in. Men on horseback broadcast bulbous bluegrass seed all over the mountain. I'm told they put socks over the ears of their horses, put "airplane seeders," as they called them, around their necks, and went up and down these ridges scattering seed. That must have been a whale of a job! By comparison, airplane seeding is cheap.

Right away after we started the job, we reseeded a lot of the logged areas next to the road all the way around the loop. We worked on foot with an old crank-turn "air-plane" seeder. Jessie Goodwin helped us to do a lot of it.

For the nine years we worked the mountain, we reseeded, the grass came up, and we made sure it did not get overgrazed. It looked like a park. Unfortunately, it looks like a sand dune now in some of those areas where the people in charge have let it get overgrazed and trampled on again.

Once in a while the Forest Service put the seed on the ground using an airplane. The Association asked me to meet the crop duster in Weiser at four in the morning one year and ride with him to show him where we wanted the seed. I was not gung-ho about riding with a crop duster, but Dave Bivens insisted.

Finally I asked, "How old is this guy?"

"About seventy."

I laughed and said, "I'll go because there's no such thing as an old, bold careless crop duster."

We flew in a regular Cessna, and the ride was great. He was a good pilot, pointed things out that he was familiar with, and buzzed by my cow camp, cabin, and corrals. I really enjoyed that. I could see where my cows were and got some nice pictures.

Several times if the weather was right we put seed on after our summer's work was over. We would go to the cow camp, get the seed, go up the mountain and put it on. We weren't paid for this, since by then our contract had ended a month or six weeks before, but we wanted to see the improvement and make the country look good. We also wanted to make the Association, the permittees and the Forest Service look good.

There were several drought years, from 1977 to 1979 especially. We had little feed at the ranch or the middle pastures, but there was still a lot of feed on The Mountain. One of the best years I ever saw up top was 1977, and it was a good thing since it was so dry everywhere else. The grass up there was four feet high! The Forest Service let us move cattle to the top in July. I have pictures of me on a tall horse with the grass up above my stirrups, clear to my knees in a lot of places.

We put every cow up top that we could get our hands on. A hunter or hiker called the Forest Service and said, "Hey, all the grass is gone. It is a dust bowl up top."

The Forest Service got a hold of the Association president, Kenneth Uhrig, who told me later, "My heart just sank. I had ridden out into there from my other allotment. I knew you kept the salt out all season, more salt than we had ever had up there, and I knew how many cattle you had up there. You had most of them. I figured I was going to take a whipping that day. I agreed to meet the Forest Service, and two or three of us rode up there. There were places where there was still grass to the stirrups, and grass anywhere you looked to the horses' knees and above."

Apparently the hunter had seen a salt ground where the grass doesn't grow great and wanted to stir up trouble. There was plenty of feed left on the meadows up there. If I'd had some way to cut it, bale it, and put it in my hay barn, I wouldn't have had to buy hay for several years for my horses.

With conditions so dry in 1979, the associations for miles around us, not just the nearby ones, had to pull their cattle off The Mountain in August. They kept saying there was no feed. Dave Bivens asked us, "What's it like up top? Do we need to think about pulling them off?" I was astounded, and so was Bev. There was feed up there to the cows' knees, and we knew it—hundreds of acres.

The next week he talked to me again. "I'm getting a lot of static from these other associations, and they're saying they're having to pull their cattle off."

I said, "Dave, there is feed. You don't have to worry. Take my word for it."

"I'd like some pictures to chuck down these guys' throats."

Bev and I rode up to check the salt and the cattle, took my camera and a white measuring tape. We went out in the scabby parts, we went in the good parts, we took pictures and gave the film to Dave. And we left cattle up there the rest of the summer. If you take care of the grass, it will take care of you in a crunch.

We bought horse hay from Bev's dad for a few years. Then we met Frank and Elizabeth Cada in Crane Creek. They lived on the corner going into Weiser one direction and to North Crane the other. The little schoolhouse still sits on the corner where Elizabeth came to teach school as a young woman. She met and married Frank and moved across the road into Frank's house where they raised their family. They were there a long time before they sold their place and moved into Weiser because of Frank's illness.

When we started buying hay from the Cadas, Frank insisted that his hired man would load our truck. My truck had bows over the top the full length of it and a forty-inch door at the end of it, so they couldn't just pick up the bales and drop them in.

Their hay accumulator could pick up and deliver eight bales at a time, but to load us was a lot of hand work. It cost Frank money to have his hired man put sixty-some bales in that truck and then load the pickup. But Frank just laughed and stood around jawing with us and the men and made sure the job got done right.

He always left word for his help. "When you see Carol and Bev's truck comin', if I'm not here, you're to be out of that field and meet 'em at such and such a haystack."

Elizabeth always expected us to come in and have a cold drink with her and sit and cool off while the men were loading the hay for us.

It usually took us at least two days to haul the hay we needed because we always kept a ton or two in the shed over the winter. Elizabeth would insist that we come back the second day and eat lunch with them, and it would be roast beef and all the trimmings. One year it was roast moose. She loved to cook and always had a hay crew to cook for. They were a grand couple.

Talking about Elizabeth's food gets me thinking about the food Bev and I enjoyed while we were on the job. Makes me hungry!

We have been asked, "Who does all the cooking?"

I just laugh. "Whoever's the least poopdest when we came in after an all-day jaunt on a horse, instead of three hours like we've been with you. Whoever gets the hungriest and can wiggle the firstest is mostest in the kitchen for that meal."

The first year or two we saw more men on this mountain than we did the last seven years. Maybe they couldn't quite figure out how women could do this job. They stopped by to pass the time of day with us and ask, "Well, what did you have for breakfast this morning?"

"Sourdough waffles and fresh strawberries and whipped cream," we might say.

That would just blow their mind. "In a cow camp?"

I cooked the waffles on an old waffle iron with willow handles that came across the prairies with my grandmother. I kept burning those handles out on my gas range, so I replaced them with permanent steel rods. I figured heated-up handles are better than burned-out ones!

I planted strawberries in my front terraces along with flowers. I did not have to bend over very far to pick the strawberries, and whenever I watered the flowers, I watered the strawberries. We had a propane refrigerator, so we could keep whipped cream or whatever we wanted.

Bev and I both love ice cream. Our friends Denny and Joy Weaver down the canyon made homemade ice cream like my mother used to make, creamy and super good. We loved eating homemade ice cream with them.

Another thing that we liked to eat was huckleberries. We picked enough to keep in the refrigerator for huckleberry hotcakes and muffins.

We made chocolate pudding, chocolate pie, strawberry pie, or raspberry pie (also from the garden) and topped them off with whipped cream. We always had fresh fruit around. We took oranges in our saddlebags when we were going on cattle drives so we wouldn't have to get off our horses to get a drink.

I'm not a big fish eater, but we fished some in the evenings if we had time. We always seemed to have fences to put in across the creek. My favorite philosophy was, "You have to test the water for crocodiles and alligators before you get out in that creek to put the creek crossings in. You test for crocodiles and alligators with a fly pole."

Wild mushrooms were prolific some years. We would come home with salt sacks on a pack horse full of cauliflower mushrooms or morels. There were acres of them. I canned a lot of mushrooms some years.

As I've already noted, 1977 was the driest year on record. We were supposed to be on the Bear Creek side in 1977, our first year. It was so dry that there was very little water on the Bear Creek side, and certainly not enough for over five hundred head of cows and their calves. They had us put them over on the Third Fork side, which threw us out of sync with the rotation for Ola "C." The year we were on Third Fork, which was our south side, Ola "C" was down on their south end. The next year we started out on our north side and Ola "C" came to their north boundary—Third Fork Creek. Normally it worked out well and gave the pastures some need rest and rotation. When it was too dry we had to run a pump out of Squaw Creek to have water in the corrals and to the house.

We had a lot of lightning and a lot of thunderstorms. During one lightning storm we were coming down out of the mouth of Squaw Creek Canyon out into the Pole Creek area and had just hit a logging road. A bolt of lightning hit the ridge a few hundred yards in front of us.

Those horses fell to their knees, and my heart went right with them.

Once the lightning struck where we had horses turned out in the pasture up north of the house where there is a big rocky cut in the road, probably fifty, sixty feet high. It slants just a little, enough so that if a horse was catty enough, she could "walk" down off of it. My horse that tried that broke her neck eventually, but most of the horses wouldn't even try it.

We had a fantastic thunder and lightning show one night. Next morning we saw two battered horses on the road, old Dutch and Rosey. They had come off of that hill on a dead run from the looks of things and had skidded at the last moment. They had kept on going over that almost sheer cliff and rolled. They were both bruised and skinned and looked like someone had taken a whip to them and clipped their hide all over. They were sore—and worthless for a while. We had some close hits that night. If we had known the lightning storm was coming, we would have kept them in the corral.

Another time in early July I was in the middle of the creek fixing fence when a downpour hit us. There was lightning all around, and that's just where you don't want to be in a lightning storm. You're out in the middle of ice-cold, swift, snow-melt water up to your belt. You've got two wires strung across the creek and the third one in your hand, and then this thunder and lightning hits and then the downpour. Your whole life goes before you pretty fast.

In the summer of 1978 we knew it had been a hard winter because there was a lot of snow up the West Mountain canyon trail, with snowdrifts four feet high. Looking down into Miner's Flat, we could see it was snow white. And this was early July. Lots of snow.

Summer can get scorching hot on the mountain. My house sits in the bottom of Bear Creek Canyon, in timber, and there's always a breeze. I have a bed fixed so that it's up high. Lying on that bed, your whole body's up above the railing on the porch. You're always catching a breeze.

But it was ninety-eight degrees on the porch that summer, the highest temperature I can remember. We were usually ten to fifteen degrees cooler than it was in Boise. If we turned a radio on in the pickup and found out it was ninety-eight where we were on the mountain, we knew we could add at least ten degrees and that's what it was in Boise.

The earliest snow on record was August 13, 1978. We had cattle up top. We had barely gotten them up there, and we got a snow that turned the high country white. The line cabin up there has some interesting writing on the walls. Penciled on the wall is the earliest day the snow fell each year. Our record stood clear into 1985 when we quit keeping track, but I don't believe it's come any earlier since then.

That snowstorm shot cows off the mountain when it was about time for us to go to school. We had our hands full getting them back up.

Another time we were in the valley picking up Betty Crow, a college friend. When we came back a big tree, probably two feet through at the butt, had fallen. The middle of the tree landed across the corral and broke all the two-by-eight panels. Then the tree slid across the road and blocked it off, knocking the top pole off the fence on the corrals opposite it. We had a corral fixing spree not to mention cutting that log. Nobody could get around it. People who came that far but didn't have a saw with them had to go back the way they came because we weren't there to cut it out.

On June 12 and 13, 1981, we had snow at five thousand feet up at the old spring. Snow on July 9, 1981 up at Green Field flats riddled the False Hellbore growing there. This plant has a large leaf like the corn leaf except that it's about six inches wide and a foot long or better. The storm riddled those leaves like you had taken a knife and worked it down each vein. My garden froze in early September of 1982, and there was snow on top September 12 that year.

CHAPTER 16

STORIES TOLD OUT OF SCHOOL

FROM THE TIME I STARTED TEACHING in 1962, I was the sponsor of the Girls' Athletic Association and taught physical education as well as biology. I worked four years at Wilder High School, Wilder, Idaho and made many lifelong friends. In search of greener pastures I took a P.E. and coaching job at Adrian High School, Adrian, Oregon, in 1966. I taught a lot of different classes and coached many different girls' sports in the twenty-nine years I taught there. You make many lifelong friends when you stay in one place that long.

Every year we brought some girls who wanted to come up to the ranch. Genetty Piercy came along faithfully each year to hold down "the camp" when we were gone all day.

The girls always enjoyed themselves and wanted to stay longer. In the spring I was busy trying to fix fence and get ready for cattle. "If you want to stay for or five days," I told the girls, "I'll make a deal with you. You help me one day, and then I'll take the rest of the time and take you on a big hike and do whatever else you want me to do."

They agreed, and it worked well as long as the kids knew what they were getting into.

One time I took them on an all-day hike fifteen miles into the deep snow that was so hard we could walk on it. We were clear up onto the bottom of Gabe's Peak and over to Wilson Mountain.

We were cutting through the country and couldn't follow any trails. As we came to a rest at some aspen groves, the kids said, "Let's carve our initials."

I carved in AHS (for Adrian High School) and the date, and the kids put their initials in the tree. Fifteen years later when I was chasing wild cows for the cattle association on Wilson Mountain, I saw that tree, and it brought back a lot of memories. It was dead, but you could still see the initials and dates.

Before the kids came up I would get the dirt out of the cabin. Sometimes the girls would come up and help. One girl, Mary Looney, was a good worker and her mom was glad to let her go, especially when she found out she was going to help clean house.

She said, "Good. Maybe Mary will learn to clean house, because I sure can't get much out of her here."

Mary had the last laugh. She was good help. The cabin had a cement floor and a newly painted ceiling with solid wood paneling on the walls. I brought in the hose. We squirted a little cold spring water and soap on the ceiling and washed it down. Then we washed the walls down the same way and scrubbed the fireplace.

We turned the hose on the floor and let the water run out the front door. As soon as it dried, the house was clean.

That trip we had some really great girls with us. They were big jokers who could hand it out as well as take it.

The girls liked to keep an eye on me. They weren't about to go outside at night if they couldn't see where I was. They were almost as afraid to go out alone as they were nervous about going out if I was already out there.

One night I sneaked out on them. I figured, "Sooner or later, they've got to come out and go up to the outhouse." Sooner or later never came. They had their fingers crossed, their eyes crossed, their legs and toes crossed, but they never budged.

I thought, "I'll fix you guys." I crawled up on the ladder (I had been fixing the fireplace chimney before they got there) and put a piece of steel across the top of the fireplace. I had stoked the fire up before I had left. They took clothes off and kept fanning as it started to smoke. My paint job got pretty black, but it was worth it to watch and hear them.

They were gasping and talking and saying things. Pretty soon they had all the windows open. I squirted a little water here and there or scratched on the screen to scare them. They finally got down on the floor to get away from the smoke. When they came out, I had them where I wanted them.

Another time I had the girls staying at the rock house at the main ranch a mile away. This was before I got the cabin finished

I had them all bedded down outside the house, their heads up close to the house to keep out of the wind. They thought I had gone to bed over at Bear Creek.

About an hour later I got the hose and squirted some water on the roof and let it dribble down on their side. They thought it was raining, and they kept burying themselves in their blankets. I heard them talking about when they ought to get up and come into the house. I threw a set of big horse hobbles with a chain and swivel in the middle up onto the roof. It made an awful noise on that steel roof. I screamed and yelled. They came out of their sleeping bags. Everything was flying.

One year the weather opened up pretty good early in the summer at the lower country at four to five thousand feet. I took them on an all-day hike clear up to Wilson Meadows, up in Alpine country.

We took along two or three plastic toboggans we could roll up and stick under our arms. They slide along fast on that hard snow. We packed our lunches and hiked up to Third Fork Ridge, Gabe's Peak, and clear into Wilson Meadows. There was so much snow we could stand on the snow and sit on the roof of the cabin at the cow camp there.

Coming back, we cut across some cougar tracks on the trail that we had made in the snow coming up. Some of us saw a cougar as we slid off Gabes Peak.

One year the girls all bedded down at Bear Creek in the horse pasture across from the cabin. This was before I built the rawhide shack and the tack shed in the middle of nowhere. The full moon came up. A breeze made the timber squeak. The coyotes howled.

I got the girls down in their sleeping bags. I had a recording with actual wolf howls on it, and Bev played it on her portable tape recorder. About one o'clock in the morning I sent Bev down to the main road and gate to play that recording. We put on our dark blue sweatsuits so we would blend in better. The moaning of the wolf started as the moon came up over the high ridge. The owls were hooting, the coyotes were howling, and the timber was squawking.

I was sleeping out on the porch and could hear the girls talking. Some of them wanted to get up and run. Some of them wanted to stay. Some of them said, "We're gonna get ate no matter what 'cause it's too far from the house."

I thought, "I had better speed things up here a little." I had a 410 shotgun, so I reached up and shot it in the air and shouted, "I got him! I got him!"

By that time you could hear the girls coming up the pasture, and there's a log footbridge over the creek. They came faster than I thought they would.

Halfway down the driveway the drawstring on my sweatpants broke. I let them fall down around my knees, and I fell down in the gravel. I knew I had to get up and get out of there before they saw me because they had flashlights. I managed to get down to the gate holding onto my sweatpants with one hand and my gun in the other. I shot one more time and distracted them. They all bounded into the cabin. Bev and I kept our faces straight.

They wanted to know where I had been. "Well, I shot one of them down at the gate," I said and let it go at that.

They were in their undies and outies and next to nothings. All their sleeping bags and clothes were over in the horse pasture. They weren't about to go back and get them.

I said, "I'm not going to go over there and get them for you. You guys go get 'em."

Three of the bravest said, "We'll go if you'll go with us and bring your shotgun." By then it was two o'clock in the morning. I built a big fire up, and three or four of us went over. I came behind them with the shotgun, the big outrider here. There was undies and outies scattered on the bushes and fences and everywhere through that pasture. There were some in the draw the next morning that fell off them as they were coming across the bridge.

We got everything picked up and they started back. They got to the garden and almost to the bridge, and I shot in the air again. They took off a hundred miles an hour, got to the house and slammed the door. I liked to never got it open when I reached the house. We got them settled down on the floor, more logs on the fire. It was hot in there.

Bev and I went back to our sleeping bags on the porch. "You know, we're going to build fence through that main gate tomorrow. We're never going to get those girls out there. We've got to get these "wolves' up the canyon," I told Bev.

I asked her to go back behind the woodshed with her tape recorder, make it loud and then ease it off like he's going up there through the timber.

I always had a mother come up with me. Genetty Piercy was with me on this trip. She had a heart condition and stayed in the bunkhouse. I had told her earlier that there would be plenty of mayhem and lots of noise and not to worry about it.

She said it was quite interesting, taking it all in at two o'clock in the morning.

Next morning it was bright and sunny. Margo and another girl decided to go down to the gate to see what that wolf was about that I had supposedly shot a few hours before.

I was on the spot. I said, "The wolf is either dead or injured, and the other wolves will take him away. Won't be anything. Might be some blood."

I had forgotten I had been using bright red stain for my gates, and there was stain in the ground from that.

When they came back, their eyes as big as their heads, they said they could see where there had been a fight, that the road was scuffed up and there was blood everywhere.

When I first started teaching, at Wilder, Idaho, the kids wanted to come up. I said, "Fine. Bring one of your moms." We got some transportation, and a few of them came up. They stayed in the rock house.

We picked up a bull snake about three and a half or four feet long that had been hit in the road. It was in perfect condition, just his head was flat.

I swore Sue Norris and Bev Lowe, who were with me, to absolute secrecy, and I hid that snake. That night the kids wanted to hear ghost stories. We sat around the fireplace and ate popcorn. I salted it extra heavy so they would want more lemonade and pop to drink. About one o'clock in the morning I got them bedded in.

The kids were scared of the ghosts and put the chairs in the narrow part of the house between the cookstove and the stairwell, a pretty good barricade.

Bev Lowe and Angie slept in a big bed by the door. When the door opened, you could only see half the bed. I told Bev, "I've got a score or two to settle with Angie, and I'm going to do it tonight. Get her in her sleeping bag, and her arms zipped in. I don't care how."

I told the kids, "I need your flashlights." I put them all on the table. I said, "If you have to get up in the night, you know where they're at."

They fell for that. I scooped up the dishpan I had them in and took them with me. All they had was a little firelight.

They were dozing off when I came back in and threw that door open with a loud noise and hollered out, "Who's got my bird book?" (Who needs a bird book at 1:30 in the morning?) I had the snake in my left hand. Angie and Bev were on my left side as I burst into the house. I heaved that big, dead snake backhand towards the bed the two girls were in. I had no idea Angie would sit straight up in bed or I would not have done this. That cold, wild snake wrapped around her neck like a whip!

The sleeping bag lost its zipper and she came out of it like a bullet—ripping the snake off her neck and out the door she came! I knew I was dead meat if she ever caught me!

There was a four-wire fence around there, and I went over it like a bullet. Angie couldn't make it over the fence. She had to let the gate down to get through. That extra second gave me the time I needed, and I was long gone toward Bear Creek by the time she got through the fence. She threw the snake after me.

After things quieted down, I went back and got the snake and went to the outhouse. I wrapped the snake around the toilet seat in that one-holer. The door wouldn't shut on that dilapidated old building. I settled back in the brush to listen. It wasn't long before somebody needed to go to the bathroom. They didn't know where I was and couldn't find the flashlights since I still had them. Finally, two of the girls got there. No lights. Somebody sat down with her bare behind on that cold slimy snake. That outhouse shook, rattled, and rolled. The biggest earthquake around. I just lay on the ground and rolled, laughing.

For Advanced Biology you had to be a junior or senior. You could take it both years and do the field trip twice.

My main prankster buddy was Doc Hyde, a veterinarian in Emmett. He was a big joker who liked kids. He came over to Adrian High School every year to talk about being a vet and share stories.

He could outrun any of our kids even in his cowboy boots. He was not a big man and did not make a very big hole in the brush when he had the kids following him on some wild goose chase. Orville and Aloisa Harris, Jessie Goodwin and Norma Hyde were all good help on many trips. Lupe Castro's husband, Mike, was my male chaperone for years—missing only one year. He would take vacation time to be able to come on those field trips.

The kitchen crew at Adrian High School also helped. Zelma Ocamica and Doreen Bingham were the head cooks down through the years. They would fill white buckets of kitchen-made chocolate chip cookies and send them, ten to thirty dozen cookies, in those buckets.

I always told my students that this field trip was a privilege, not a right.

They had to behave in class throughout the year with a grade of a C or better, be passing in all their subjects and have an OK from all their other teachers. Some of them didn't make the grade. Word got around that the gray-haired biologist would make them stay home if they didn't have their work done.

They studied a lot of botany on these field trips: plant identification, collecting and learning to press flowers and writing scientific tags for them, learning the uses of the plants, range uses, and poisonous plants—the good, the bad, and the ugly.

They also studied a lot of ecology, ornithology, mammology, geology, weather and clouds, and astronomy. They studied stream flow, speed and load. They did population studies with layout grids. They did a lot of logging and ranching and environmental studies. They learned to look at the situation the way an environmentalist might see it. They looked at the ethics of things. They learned how to take field notes and learned observation skills.

The final test of the year was a walk-through test with 150-175 points on a good year. I would ask a question. The students would write it down on a clipboard, and then we would turn around and discuss it right away. Then I would take the senior biology students for a more extended test.

The first trip there weren't very many kids. I just had the house and porch and not a lot of room.

We woke up the next morning with six inches of wet snow on the ground, and huge flakes floating down. We kicked the snow off the flowers to "do our botany."

After the field trip I would tell the students not to talk much about Doc's part of the trip. We would get them every time, but we didn't want them to spill the beans back home to the other students or even to their family, because they had brothers and sisters coming up.

For years nobody ever told the stories of what happened. They always said, "You'll never get me again."

I had the second year students in my hip pocket. I told them to play along with the joke. Fear seems to lead to more fear and always their make-believe fear leads to real fear—it never failed.

Doc would bring his red-bone hounds with him on a Tuesday night, and then he would auction off his hounds to the kids for up to two dollars they could bid on a dog. This went back to the pot to buy milkshakes. Usually Doc did not like other people handling his dogs. That way they stayed loyal to him and only had one "boss" to obey. But he went out of his way to let the kids on our field trips handle and be around his hounds.

After the auction Doc would lay a long scent trail to a tree with something up it. The kid would have to go up and try to retrieve his hound if his dog bayed first. Doc would say, "Old Duke bayed first. Who's got Duke?" The kid would have to go pull off the dog from the tree, and that could be pretty traumatic, trailing that dog for maybe an hour through swamp and trees and then pulling him off a supposed lion or bear or something.

I asked, "What are we going to do about flashlights, Doc? We can't have those around."

"I'll take care of that," he said. He would tell the kids before we left, "Leave all your flashlights on the van or on the bus."

The kids would say, "Why?"

"When these dogs tree and you shine that light up the tree on that critter, he's going to come right down that flashlight path and right at you."

He had them so scared by then that they believed him, and they would all stash their flashlights. Doc would be the only one with a flashlight.

They would take off to heck and begone, over the mountains, through the brush, over the rocks, in the swamps, over the creek bottoms, through the small creeks and around the trees, in the timber, and you name it. They would follow him like a puppy dog, on the double.

The maps tell you the ranch is located in the foothills of the Rockies. There's a lot of terrain to cover. Doc wasn't hunting anything, but he would start out with the kids after dark—pitch dark unless there was moonlight, which made it even scarier.

If there was a little breeze, that would make the trees rub together and make them squeak and squawk and howl. The creeks would roar by, and a jet going by overhead might make a roar or rumble. There was just some little noise constantly going on besides what the kids were trying to hear, and the dogs baying. It was an exhilarating experience.

I could never keep up with them, needless to say. I would wait for them to catch up with me on the horse or the ATV and then go with them a ways, and then I would shut the lights off. I didn't want someone coming after me!

One day I had a roll of horse hide soaking in Bear Creek. When I got up that first morning, I went down to the creek to retrieve the rawhide and a hungry bear had really and truly chewed a lot of that rawhide up.

I knew a bear had been there all week turning over tree stumps and eating ants. It was kind of interesting to the students, after all, they were on Bear Creek.

Doc has a son who's a taxidermist and he did a bobcat that looks like a great big tabby lying in front of the fire. Doc would climb up a tree and put this cat on a limb. The kids could see it, but they had a hard time telling it wasn't for real.

He took those kids through some of my creek-bottom meadows where there are swamps, muck holes, brush, fences, grass to your knees; they were a sorry-looking sight by the time they climbed through everything.

By the time they got back to the road they were about as slimy as those mud holes they would come through, and Doc was up on the hill above them. I would count noses to make sure they had all got to the road.

Doc was yelling at them, "C'mon! The dogs are gonna tree pretty soon!" They scrambled after the dogs, and here they were baying up at this tree.

Doc shone his light up just enough so they could see his bobcat. A third or half of these kids every year are in my taxidermy class, some in their third year. They have "stuffed" bobcats, cougars, bears, and done all sorts of things. They know what glass eyes look like. But their eyes are so glassed up from being loaded up with adrenaline that they forget common sense, and they really get took.

Spike had to crawl up that tree (since it was his dog that treed), so when he was eyeball-to-eyeball with that cat, he realized it wasn't real, but he didn't let on. Finally Doc told him, "Kick that thing out of there!"

The kids took off out into the brush. Spike kicked it and acted like he was really scared. When it landed of course everyone caught on, so we walked up to the cabin for hot sourdough doughnuts at 12:30 in the morning.

Another year Doc put the bobcat into the big A-framed birch-lined two-holer outhouse at my cabin while the kids were all indoors. They couldn't see it when they first went in there. Of course no one needed to go there that night!

Finally I took a senior girl to the side and told her to take another girl with her to the outhouse. "Make sure she goes in there first, and then you shine the light in for her."

They came into the house yelling and screaming bloody murder, and that kid was as white as a sheet. I always thanked Rolinda for that little trick; she was such an actress!

Doc's son Brent, a game warden, used to come up and talk about his career and answer questions. He was as a good a prankster as his dad. One day his beeper went off, and he went back to his pickup. When he came back he told his dad that he had picked up a radio message. "I don't know if you ought to take these kids runnin' tonight or not," he said. "That radio message was there are out-of-staters up here, and they've wounded a sow and her cub. She's up on the ridge headed this way. I've got a game warden up there trying to find the bear and the cub. The bear has chewed up one guy pretty good. They may have to airlift him out of here. I just don't know about going up there tonight with these kids." All this was said with dead serious voices and faces.

The kids were disappointed, of course. Doc could put a good face on it all. We decided we could just go around the cabin. Doc and Mike laid a trail and went up behind the house in the big meadow back there and up on the ridge and circled back, hit another trail and went up Bear Creek a ways and them came back down through some brush and awful timber to just about a hundred and fifty yards from the house.

Doc got started with the kids and the dogs took off on another trail. Doc took the boys and outran them all in the dark— running down his hounds. In the meantime it had rained a little and the scent trail Mike and Doc had laid down earlier had gone cold. Doc put scent on the soles of Mike's boots and told him to run ahead of the dogs. He had the dogs all on leashes, so Mike was safe. Mike was making good time and somehow a dog got loose from its kid handler and took off. The chase was on!

The kids ended up in a brushy, downed timber area with the dogs baying that they had treed. A taxidermist can fix up some fun things, and the sound of a hissing and spitting critter can shake the best of them up!

The kids didn't know what was there making a lot of noise in the hawthorne patch. We never did tip our hands, and Doc finally called the kids off. They were scared because it sounded like a bear.

They came back to the house, and we had refreshments. Doc and his son were talking about what they were going to do next. "You've got to bring those hounds back in the morning," Brent said, "and help the game department find that wounded bear."

Doc said, "I can't. I have a horse surgery in the morning."

His son twisted his arm, and the kids took all that in. They never did realize what was up. They were sure a bear was still running wild. We did not go up Bear Creek the next day, just to keep them in the dark.

Another trip, Doc and I had a pretty good one planned. When I got up there on a week end, I found that someone had broken into my cabin, twisted the doorknobs and had gone through everything. I don't know what they were looking for, but whatever it was I guess I didn't have. I had to finish twisting the front doorknob off to get in they had jammed it so bad.

We stayed at the lower ranch until the kids got here. The sheriff told me there had been two walkaways from the juvenile facility near Sweet, and they might be the ones who had done the break-in. The Forest Service work camp had been broken into, and a lot of things stolen. So they were out casting for some hard characters.

I told the kids this. I knew the Forest Service had a work crew of about twenty men from the state pen, but I thought it would be after the kids and I were in there.

The second night a big blond fellow walked up the lane. I had never seen him before. He strode up through the terraces like they were steps and told me who he was. That didn't mean anything to me. He told me where he was staying, and then I knew who he was, the crew boss for the convict crew. The kids picked up on that.

Here we had a break-in at my place, a break-in at the Forest Service, and two walkaways from the juvenile center, and some other things, so the kids were shook up.

Earlier I had told Brian, a neighbor kid, to come along in the evening, to "just be there." I told him, "The kids will have some free time, playing frisbies or something, and I don't want them to see you. I just want you to be a presence."

So that's what he did. He threw a wet pine cone or two and threw a rock or two, groaned a little. He drove a yellow pickup as did the guy who had pulled a gun on the schoolbus a year or two before. The kids hadn't forgotten that.

Brian drove by in a yellow pickup. The kids' ears went up immediately. When Brian got up on the hill, one group of kids thought it was the other group making the noise, and vice versa. Finally they got their heads together and found it wasn't either one of them, and they ended up over at the house.

Mike went down with Doc to the white house where Doc stays on the middle ranch when he's up here, and they thoroughly and carefully trashed that house inside. They turned pictures upside down, tipped the lamp and chairs over, messed the beds up, turned the table over. Doc had drawn a huge syringe of blood from his horse, and he squirted that into the white porcelain sink and on the doorstep and the pole. He put blood toward the outhouse and under it.

Mike came back really excited, calling my name and saying, "Doc needs you! Doc needs you!"

"I can't go down there," I told him. "I've got all these kids."

"Doc says he has to have you. There's been a shootin' and they've broken into the house. They've trashed it, and they're going to need some first aid if they ever find the guy that's been shot. You're a first-aid instructor, and you've got to come." (Never mind that Doc is a veterinarian.)

I told the kids, "Each one of you find a club or a weapon of some kind. You boys, remember, the first priority is the girls—and Carol, our bus driver. The girls are to be in the middle of the group with you boys surrounding them."

I drove my own pickup down. They got down to the bus with their sticks and shovels and lead pipes and you name it. I didn't know I had lead pipe on the place, but next day I found several. They got down to the hill, and Carol pulled over. I started over toward the bus, and here came a pair of headlights. I had no idea who that was.

I always knew who was on the creek. I kept track, just in case someone got foxy.

I stepped away from the bus to see what was going on and here came a yellow pickup! Even I was a little taken back by that! It was Brian. His headlights shined up on the bus. As I turned around the full glass door and entrance well and steps were stacked full of what looked like a bunch of Zulu warriors. They all had their sticks, shovels, pipes and clubs ready for mayhem. Carol told me later, "If that yellow pickup had stopped, I couldn't have held the door shut. They were looking for revenge."

Brian kept going. The kids had to walk three-quarters of a mile to the house. My pickup was not Oregon-certified to haul kids, so I had a good excuse not to take them with me. They had to walk down there and then all the way back up.

It was dark, of course.

Doc said, "I don't know. It's pretty bad. I'm not sure if we should go or not."

We bickered back and forth for a while. The place was thoroughly trashed. The year before someone had put a bullet hole through the door. If Doc had been sitting at the table it would have gone through one ear and out the other. The hole was still big enough you could stick a ball point pen through it. Most of the kids hadn't seen that the year before.

The kids got over to the house and couldn't believe the mayhem and blood.

Once I had a lot of football players in my group, and this "macho" thing was running deep. Doc came up early with his hounds and horse and looked around to see where he wanted to lay his trail.

He had run into a bear a time or two during the day, so he made a trail to heck and begone again clear out in the forest and back to where I was and then out to the Forest Service road again, up through the rocks and the brush, steep. Away the kids went. We started about 11:30 that night. I wanted to wait until the moon came up.

Doc had just done an autopsy of a horse, and the pictures were gory and coarse. He had shown them to the kids while they were having dinner, and he told them that was what was left of a man that a bear had killed. He said that the law had called him in with his hounds to help run that bear and that was what he was running tonight.

About 11 p.m. when the moon had appeared over the ridge the kids left the vans down by the rock house. Doc ran those kids all over the place and finally got back to the bear rug. With no flashlight on and Mike in the brush growling and hitting the brush with a stick, it was pretty realistic. Especially when the dogs bayed "treed" and doc shined a small light on the fangs and mouth of the bear rug! The kids took off and Doc had to gather them all up and head north behind his hounds. He told the biggest boys who were football players—"You stay behind the girls and I don't want you anywhere else!" They knew he was dead serious when he gave them the flashlight.

The kids and Doc got to the bear tree before I did. The dogs were going wild and trying to climb up in the tree. When I arrived

Doc disappeared for awhile. One of the girls said, "Look up there. That bear has moved up the tree ten feet since we got here!"

I told her I would be more worried about where that bear's mother was—"I think that was his mother back there in the brush from the sounds of it!"

I eventually got them all headed back south towards Mike. He put on a hissing, spitting, growling fit when they got close. They all had their flashlights on by now and when they heard "the bear" (Mike) they took off running toward the vans.

We got them loaded up and out the main gate. There was no Mike or Doc, so I told them not to lock the gate. That was the first time they had missed Mike.

"Where's Mike" they asked.

"Aw, he's back there with Doc, helping get the dogs together. They'll be around."

Eventually they came. "We don't have to tip our hand," I told Doc. "Bring that tree-climbing bear and set it on that can of dog food there by the door."

So the kids still had that in their minds.

After we had all enjoyed our sourdough donuts and s'mores, Mike and Doc showed up. Doc said to the girls, "I've got some stuff down in the pickup. Would one of you girls mind going and getting it?"

Marilee said, "Sure," and took off.

The football players sitting by the door didn't budge. Marilee went outside, banging the screen door and ran head-on into that bear. She started screaming and jumping up and down. She tried to grab that screen door to get back in, but she couldn't get it open.

The boys were sitting six inches from the main door, and they wouldn't even lift a hand to open that door and let her in. They just scooted further under the table. She was screaming. Finally she got the door open and ran inside.

She was wearing a silly type of hat. She jumped up and down so hard the hat went up, she went down, and as she jumped back up, her hat connected to her head again—all in mid-air. I was laughing hard. Doc went out and grabbed the bear and set it on a table.

Another time a biker died in an accident. I saw his obituary in the Caldwell newspaper, and it said he would be buried in Ola. I thought, "That's strange. You just don't go up and say you want somebody to be buried in Ola. You have to go through a committee, and more than likely you aren't going to get the privilege."

I said, "There's going to be a story here." This was the week before my field trip that year.

When we got to the ranch, a neighbor said, "Yes! Karen was on her tractor going to the hayfield when a procession of black Cadillacs came by followed by an entourage of bikers with all their leather and chains."

She just about swallowed her teeth and sat on her tractor until they went by the lane. She decided she wasn't going anywhere and went back to the house.

Within about thirty minutes they came back. When I heard that, I thought, "Well, there go the plans Doc and I had. We've got to go on this instead." My mind started working overtime. I came up with a story that the kids have never forgotten.

I cleaned the rawhide shack up, took the ashes out of the stove and dumped most of them where the kids couldn't see them. I mashed chicken bones to splinters and mixed them with ashes and dumped them in plain sight on their way to the outhouse at the corral.

The first night we walked around and ended up at the cow camp. The full moon was shining through the timber, and they wanted ghost stories.

I told them the biker story and said, "They were only gone thirty minutes, so they had to be right about here where they dumped those ashes. Bikers used to camp up there all the time before Dad fenced that off." (They didn't. The hunters did.) I said, "They cremated him and threw his ashes out, and, you know when they cremate a biker they cremate his bike, his Harley, with him."

Most of these kids were ranch kids and knew the tune, "Ghost Riders in the Sky." The cowboy dies and instead of going to hell he's assigned to ride the clouds chasing wild red-eyed cows forever with no rest—on a renegade horse. "That's the way these bikers are," I said. "They'll cremate his bike, and he'll ride up there with those cowboys, and you'll hear that bike."

What they would hear was the drumming of ruffed grouse in the morning. They sound just like a motorcycle trying to start and never kicking in.

"I don't know where they scattered the ashes," I said, "but while we're picking flowers and doing geology, we'll probably see them somewhere."

Now they were in our hip pockets.

Next morning we fed the girls first as usual. While I was frying eggs and fixing pancakes, here came Mike, a senior student. He sat down by the door, white as a sheet. He could hardly talk.

"What's the matter with you?" I asked.

"I-I-I heard it," he stammered.

"What did you hear?" I asked, knowing very well what he had heard.

"I heard that biker. I heard his bike!"

"Where were you?"

"I got up at the crack of dawn to go to the outhouse. When I came back I heard that motorcycle trying to start, and when I looked down, there was that pile of ashes. And there were bones in it! I heard that bike trying to start!" He was beside himself. I turned my back on him to work at the sink to keep from cracking up.

By then the other boys came over, saying that they had heard the bike, too, and saw the ashes. I never did own up to that one.

On our next-to-last field trip there was only one girl. This was in 1994. Casey was a straight-A student, fun to be around, good to help in the kitchen. It was just she and I in the house.

Doc and I set up a deal that we were going to have a cougar experience. There were cougar in the area and every now and then you would see the tracks or hear one or even see one. Doc had an older friend who was a logger and had never been up here.

The lane to the house has a dog leg in it, and if you aren't careful and go the wrong direction you'll end up in Bear Creek. Doc told this fellow, Cliff, that we would meet him at the white house. Cliff and Doc and Mike laid some scent out, and Cliff was going to stay there. He didn't want Cliff mixing with the kids.

We auctioned the dogs off, and Cliff didn't come. Doc's not a great coffee drinker, but he sat there drinking coffee until I thought his eyeballs were going to swim. Finally about 10:30 p.m. I stood up at the sink and looked down the lane.

The kids were by the fireplace. Carl, my senior aid in one of my science classes, had his Stetson on and was sitting there in one of the built-in rock seats by the fireplace, half asleep. Three of the boys, football players, went out to the porch and lay down cross-wise on the bed out there.

All at once lights came up the lane lickety-split. Nobody comes up that in daylight that fast. "I wonder where he's going to end up," I thought. He didn't know there were terraces below the house. I thought he was going to come right up through the terraces. He slammed on his brakes and left his lights on. He was a big long-legged logger. He came running up through those terraces screaming at the top of his lungs, "I need help! I need help! Cougar attack! Ate my dogs! I need help! Help! Help!" Cliff put on a real show, waving his hands and arms.

Doc had told me he wasn't going to come in for a while because he knew this was going to get good and he wanted me to enjoy it by myself.

Next thing I knew one of the football players from the bed was standing between Cliff and me with his hand on his knife (we had been digging plants). The more Cliff yelled and the more I yelled back at him, the more the kid got between us. I realized he had his machete with him, and I finally reached over, grabbed his arm and twisted it a little. He went over and sat on the bed.

Cliff and I went at it, jawing with each other. "What was he doing, disrupting my class? We don't have time for cougars."

After a bit I looked over there and wondered, "Where were the kids who were on that bed?" I was puzzled. Come to find out they had rolled off the bed into the flower bed and out of sight.

Cliff kept saying, "My granddaughter is down there, and the cougar was chewin' on her when I left. I couldn't get him off. He's eaten all my dogs. I didn't have any more shells. I need a doctor, I need an ambulance. I need a phone."

I told Cliff, "All I've got is a veterinarian. Would that do?"

"Well, I guess," Cliff huffed. (He and Doc were the best of friends.)

Finally Doc showed up. Later I asked Doc how he came out so fast. "When that little cowboy heard you raise your voice he was going to be there and handle things for you, and Cliff couldn't handle that wiry guy." Carl was small but wiry as a coiled-up spring and could clean his weight in bobcats.

Doc stepped in front of Carl and kept him inside. Eventually Doc agreed that his wife Norma would to go down the canyon to get the ambulance. That let Norma go down and get herself situated on the hill above the white house where she could hear all of this. The kids thought she was going seven miles down the canyon to call.

I got the kids around, and they got in the vans and pickups, and away they went toward the white house on the middle ranch.

As we got closer to the bridge we could hear screaming—ungodly, horrible screaming. Cliff's adult granddaughter Pam was the "victim," and she could really scream. Her screams echoed off the mountains, and the creek was roaring and the moon was halfway up in those trees, and there were some coyotes talking with all that noise, the dogs were starting to bay because they were excited.

I made them walk across the bridge and then loaded them up again and took them to within a hundred and fifty feet of the white house. Doc got the dogs out. "I don't know," he said, "This is bad."

Doc took Carl and another boy out where there was no scent trying to trail, and of course by the time he came back to where the kids were, they struck that trail he had laid and they took off.

Doc yelled down, "Carol! Get up here! Here's the granddaughter, and she's chewed up pretty bad, I don't know if she's going to live! And the dogs are treein' somewhere else. Come help her and keep the kids here while I find out what's up ahead. The cat's probably got something else up there!"

We all made up it to Pam. She was belly down in the tree duff and needles and brush, had been screaming her head off up until Doc yelled, and she was "dying" by then. There was blood (ketchup) all over her. There were no flashlights, of course, except my little penlight so I could see where I was going.

I bent down and felt her pulse and said, "Boy, this woman's dyin'. I hope Norma gets that Airflight in here quick. But then they won't come at night I don't think, it'll be an ambulance and it will take them better than an hour from Emmett. We've got to treat her for shock." It was cold that night.

So the kids all took their coats off, and threw them on top of her. I don't think Pam could have gotten up if she even wanted to.

Meantime, the dogs were baying full out up the mountain. Cliff was up there screaming, hissing, talking, and yelling at them. Doc yelled back, "Don't bring those kids up here. He just attacked somebody else and was eatin' him. But the dog's got him run off. It's too dangerous. Keep them down there! The guy's half dead!"

Cliff was screaming his head off. It sounded like mayhem royal. It was good.

What we did in 1995, my last trip, capped them all. I'd had some major surgery, and the surgeon sent me to the lower ranch to recuperate. I had a telephone if I needed help, but I was out of the stress of the valley.

I watched a lot of TV. The show they had on one channel was "Bigfoot in Idaho." One segment was about "Bigfoot above

Ola, Idaho." I about popped my stitches, and field trip plans began to form.

The TV program showed pictures over here at the cow camp on the Second Fork. It had some good pictures of the logs Bigfoot had supposedly moved back into the trail after they had been cut out of it. It was a good documentary.

I thought, "There we go!" I had six more months to think about it and conjure up what I was going to do. With my imagination, I didn't need that much time, but I had a ball with that one.

I went back to school five weeks later, and I said to the advanced biology kids, "Did anybody see that on TV?"

One girl raised her hand. I think she got laughed at so hard, she never owned up to it after that. I told them what I had seen on TV and said, "Honest to goodness. What do you think?" I played the devil's advocate. "I don't think there's anything to it."

That would let the kids use their own imaginations. For the next few months before the field trip, I kept talking like that.

Doc found some articles, copied them, and gave them to me. I haphazardly "arranged" them so the kids would see them in the cabin when we got up there...

Dave and Jeanene, our neighbors just below us, are both FedX jet pilots. They fly all over the world. They have their own bush airstrip, and they fly their own little plane also on the ranch here. They had been wanting to get in on this for a number of years, and they actually changed their schedule and cancelled a trip which meant a lot of money to them to be in on this.

I asked them, "Could you throw a rock with a message taped to it out the window when we're out over Third Fork pocket doing Botany?"

Dave laughed. "I'll do one better. Do you know what five pounds of flour looks like coming in at one hundred miles an hour? It's spectacular!"

I said, "Tape a note to it, something to the effect of Bigfoot being in the area, and that the sheriff said to be careful or something like that."

Jeanene has long, very curly hair. If she doesn't "mousse it to death" it sits out there like a bushel basket. "I won't mousse my hair. I'll get in the shower and get it wet and let it just flop." And, boy, did she look good.

We had a dry run the week before, and I sewed two sheepskins together to make a cape. Jeanene got camouflage on her face and sewed up two great big fake fur clubs for feet and hands. She looked the part. And she could screech.

We got up there with the botany kids, and the plane came over, flew around in circles, gave us a bad time. Finally he came down out of the sun, cut his engines up the hill from us a little bit and dropped a package.

The package was five pounds of flour with a note on it. The package had six ten-foot long bright orange streamers on it. It hit a rock, and flour flew like a blizzard. It was pretty impressive. Most of the note was intact, it was so well taped.

It said something about bear hunters in the area had reported to the sheriff department that a large hairy beast was in the area and that it was aggressive. "You had better be careful. Watch out. If you see anything let the Sheriff know."

The kids got shook up about that. I sent the kids straight across the ranch fence where I couldn't go with my ATV. I needed help opening the gate since the first time of the season it moves kind of tough, so Mike went with me on the ATV.

We caught up with the kids back on the ranch a while later. Those kids were up in arms about me leaving them in the middle of nowhere with all that going on. I asked Carol, the bus driver, and Michelle, one of the moms, how they kept a straight face. "I just kept marchin' north, and they followed," Carol said.

We did our botany work, got back to the reservoir at the back of the ranch where the kids dabbled in the ice cold water and cooled off. Then we went toward the rock house another two miles. We had been out by now a good share of the day, walking up one ridge and down another and everywhere else.

We finally ended up at the old wrecked bridge, which they couldn't walk because of high water (the bridge was down in the water). The bus was miles to the south.

Dave had dropped a note by the bus and we had to find that. I went ahead to the cabin to start lunch. That evening Doc came and brought Dave the pilot. I had told Doc to introduce him to me as one of his veterinary clients from the valley, which he did.

The kids had a good visit with him. They had no idea what he was up to or they would have lynched him. When they got ready to leave I said, "Mr. Merrit, why don't you take my ATV down with you? That way I won't have to ride down there in the dark in the cold."

They needed the ATV to get Jeanene up the mountain in her sheepskins and up a tree. Doc laid his scent trail off of his horse. That was one of the best trails he had ever put down.

I let it be known that we were going back to the white house again because there was no bridge on the main ranch. We started out about ten-thirty at night with the busload of kids and got down almost to the guard station.

Doc and I had arranged that we would meet at the gravel pit near the guard station, half a mile north of the middle ranch. As we came around the corner, there was Doc's outfit—his horse trailer and pickup. His grandson Shawn was there, too. He was a junior in high school and seemed very excited.

"What are you guys doing here?" I asked. "You know where you are supposed to be."

Shawn spat out, "We came around the corner and something came out of the brush right over there in the headlights. Granddad had to slam on the brakes to keep from hittin' him. It was an awful sight. Red eyes. Long hair. Terrible. It was big. Granddad said he didn't know what it was, but that was what we were going to run tonight. He said we were to wait here."

Meanwhile, Michelle (mother) proceeded to tell the kids what she knew about Bigfoot from a movie she had seen years before. This was scary.

After a while Doc came up the road on horseback. He was wearing a brand-new silver colored Stetson hat and was sitting on a dark horse. He was wearing dark clothes, except for the hat floating in the half moon. It looked like that Stetson hat was floating ten feet above the road.

He told the kids the usual things. He'd had eye surgery and couldn't run with the kids, but Shawn would run with them. Carol and Michelle wanted to go with them, and so did Dave the pilot.

They all took off up the mountainside and into old hayfields, and out in the forest, and meadows, in the gullies and up through the timber for a long time. I had already had these kids out all day running behind the ATV, and they were getting tired.

As soon as they were gone I jumped on the ATV. We got everybody up the hill. I could hear Jeanene in the tree uphill. She was chirping a little, and a dog or two would come in baying. Shawn was the only one with a flashlight, and you could see a little bit of light coming from way out in the meadow. When Jeanene saw it, she started chipping her teeth and chirping and screeching.

The kids had never been up on that side of the road before and weren't familiar with their surroundings. After a while Doc came down from the mountainside and said to me, while the kids listened in, "I don't think these kids ought to come up here. I don't know what we've got up here."

We talked a little more, and finally we agreed to let them come. "The minute I yell 'Carol, Get these kids outta here!'" he said, "I want you kids off this mountain."

I said to the kids, "After he yells that, I want you to stop at the ATV so I can count heads before we take off. I want you in my headlights." By now it was after midnight.

Doc shined the light up the mountainside. The dogs were going crazy. He shined the light just far enough to catch Jeanene's foot and some of her wild hair. She was screaming to beat all get out, chipping her teeth and really going to it. Mike was uphill snarling and hissing and beating on the brush.

The dogs were trying to grab her, and one of them did grab her foot and almost dragged her out.

Doc yelled "Carol!" and before he could get anything else out, two of the girls were already at the ATV standing there quivering. "Let's get these kids outta here," he said. By then the rest of the kids were in my headlights, but they kept going, having no idea where they were.

They didn't know there was a washed-out logging road ahead. They were just gone. The bus driver wanted to see what was going on, and I had to haul a girl or two out on the ATV. We rode down the mountain. When we got to the bottom they were all there, on the county road.

"Stay here," I said. "When Carol (bus driver) comes, I'll take her up to the bus with the ATV and then she can come down and get you."

"Oh, no! "Where you're going, we are."

"OK," I said, "start walking." I was on the ATV and had to get it up there anyway.

So they walked up the long way to the bus, and I got them settled in. After a while the bus driver, Carol, jumped in the driver's seat and told Michelle, "Get in here and shut the door. You guys should have seen what I saw. Doc let us look, and that thing bailed out of the tree and took out north."

I had told Doc I wanted Bigfoot to appear at the cabin, so it was all set. Supposedly Bigfoot was headed north with the dogs in hot pursuit.

Doc's last words to Carol (the bus driver) were, "Tell Carol (Shultz) not to wait on me. This thing's headed north. Get the kids in the cabin and keep them there. I don't know where Bigfoot's going, but he's headed that way."

Legally I couldn't let the kids drive the ATV, and they knew it, but they had bugged me all day long to let them drive or at least ride it—to no avail. It was 1:30 in the morning. I said, "Anyone want to drive the ATV?" There wasn't one finger raised up. To Carol I said, "I guess I'm going to have to drive it. I'll be right in front of your headlights. You watch, and if I think I see something and want in, you get that door open, fast, cause I'm going to be in there, new knee joint and all."

I got on the ATV and about a mile or two up the road I headed off into the meadow leading toward my cabin. I stood up on the footrest as if I had seen something that way. By then, Carol said, every kid on the bus was up trying to see what I was looking at.

Right quick I dropped on the seat, pulled my Stetson down over my ears and gunned it so hard Carol said rocks hit the windshield of the bus.

At the house I shined the lights from the ATV, and they all went into the house. The boys went to the rawhide shack to get dry clothes on, and I told them to leave the light on. I told Jeanene, Bigfoot, that if the light wasn't on, to turn it on, and if it was on, to turn it off, so they would know someone had been there.

They turned the light on and came back, and we got something to eat and settled down. It was well past one-thirty in the morning by then. We got a big fire built up. After a while Doc showed up. "I don't know where that thing went," he said, "but he's up here somewhere. You guys want to be careful."

Before long a couple of the girls who were going on a field trip in Oregon in a few days were writing reports on the bed out on the porch where their mom was sleeping.

All of a sudden, one of them came in as white as a sheet. "There's something out there, something out there!" she stammered.

"Nah, you're kidding," I said.

Bigfoot picked up a chunk of firewood and heaved it at the bottom half of the Dutch door. It rattled, and that started it off. For another hour it went like that.

Finally, the light went out in the rawhide shack. Carol said, "Did you guys leave the light on?"

"Yup."

"Well, it isn't on now," she said.

One of the girls who said she had seen Bigfoot on TV was sitting by the table. She reached up and jerked that curtain shut, and to this day that curtain doesn't work. She said, "He's not going to get me."

Things went from wild to better. The small kitchen window looks out toward the woodshed and shop, a steel corrugated building. Bigfoot got between the window light and the shop and made a big shadow. She went from one thing to another. Carol couldn't keep a straight face and had to go out on the porch to keep from laughing in front of the kids.

Two of the boys decided that if the bus driver could go out there, they could. One kid, who had been there the year before and got took, held a flashlight over his head and started out. Janine got caught by the kitchen window and squatted down behind a tree with all those sheep hides and fuzzy hair on her.

The boy walked over and saw her. Later he told me he wondered "why Shultz had so many hides out there." About then "Bigfoot" attacked him, coming up from a squat, screeching like your fingernails on the blackboard, clawing at him. The kids swore he went six feet up in the air, his feet bicycling like he was traveling a hundred miles an hour. He came straight down, and Bigfoot came

"Bigfoot" in the tree.

after him again. He jumped flat-footed across the yard, fell and cut his hand.

Doc was sitting in the house. In his dry way he said later, "I never thought I could see an entire football team come through a thirty-inch door all at the same time."

Two minutes later while some of the kids were still trying to figure it out, Bigfoot literally blew that door open like a tornado, jumped in screaming, grabbed two of the kids by the neck and held them.

A couple of kids couldn't believe this was the same creature they had seen in the tree. They described her in totally different ways. Some said she had a long tail with red eyes. Some had her with white eyes, some with no eyes. Some thought she had long body hair, and some with no hair. It was hilarious listening to them talk.

That event was Doc and Mike's finale. After that I took early retirement. I moved to the ranch and have loved every minute of my retirement since—Bigfoot and all!

Mike Castro, left, with Doc Hyde, Carol and hound.

SOME OF MY COWBOY POETRY

That Forbidden Land—The Riparian Zone

As we all know—
    The lushest grass and the plushest clover
        All love to grow where its roots can flush its feet in water.
And as we all know—
    That modern pseudo-scientist
        Commonly called an "Environmentalist"
            Thinks this lush carpet
                Was put on Earth for just one reason
                    For him and him only to romp in it all season!
It is OK if—
    He mashes the grasses till they yelp in masses
        He lets his saddle/pack stock mow the carnage
            to extend the hay he didn't want to bring from home.
    He burns U-ees with his 3-wheelers
        while his teen-age terror rips up the meadows
           with his dirt bike.
    He thinks it great sport to dam a small side stream—
        that way it floods more ground
           and makes more mosquitoes around
              and mud abounds.
        Then they both can run and spin their
           wheels through the wet meadow carnage!
    He has to dry all those muddy, wet duds,
        so he strings a line
           and strangles two spruce
    But when he goes home

somehow that line never goes with him
    and anyone horseback might lose his head
    and never get it back!
He swears at those round circles of pure nitrogen
    left by some wandering cow
    Yet he leaves far worse
        under some bush or tree
        as he never has a shovel
        And seems to string great lengths
        of unsightly paper
        Which a cow never does!
He goes home wondering why he is playing host
    to a tiny bug with a big name—*Giardia*
        gotten from the water he contaminated
        for everyone else in the watershed!
He will make a fire-ring
    most anywhere he pleases
        and when the trip is done,
            burn and maybe bury his cans and bottles
            for the next unlucky camper to find.
    Or leave a pile of his camp's garbage for the bears
        As he does not believe in the "U-Haul" system!
He may set up a few cans or bottles
    for target practice he must—no matter the
        noise and ricochet up and down the creek.
        For after all he is "shooting into a hillside!"
    But how does he know where a stray critter may be—
        whether it be fisherman, cow, deer or flower
        smeller.
    Then he is upset because there are no wild critters
        around to enjoy after his fun!
    After all—they have ears too!
He has friends coming to visit,
    so of course he must mark his camp
        and that all-purpose, recycled tree—called the
        paper plate
            is nailed to a Forest Service sign
            or a sapling trying to survive.
    On this paper plate he has all sorts of arrows and
        directions to just about everything except:
            His HOME address—cause if he did, the mail
            would deliver enough to the valley

address
to feed him all winter.
It is funny how he can get all those plates "nailed up"
But when it comes time to go home—
Both his hammer and arms must be broken
as he never takes a plate down—
They just hang like orphans—
till the winter snow
soaks them off
Like a great scab
on the countryside.
The Environmentalist likes to blame all the problems on the
Bovines—
but is blind to what *Homo Sapiens*
is doing to "his" creek!
Runoff water seems to gush down
a mountainside biketrack
much faster than through cow tracks!
And cows do not unbolt their "cutoff"
and let the exhaust
pour forth in ear-drum splitting decibels.
Cows do not put sparks out their exhaust
neither do cows drop their cigs
and matches in the forest.
Cows do not have super-hot exhaust systems
running amuck in tall, dead, dry grass.
And cows are not burning U-ees in a wet meadow—
just to see the mud and grass fly.
The Environmentalist-camper is so busy looking
for Bovine damage—he misses
"The Jeep Express" as it wallowers down the middle
of the creek in August—full of adventurous
teens, bragging
"We came all the way from the fork
of the road and never left
the creek bed!"
Over a mile of natural creekbed is torn up
and upon closer inspection—
some of those banks are knocked down
where they tried spinning
up onto the meadows.
Two days later his own terrible teen
has hot-rodded his twin carbs

all over the creek banks
     trying to see just how close he can come
      to the edge
       without caving the bank in.
And it is evident that he goofed many times,
  as there are bike track cave-ins everywhere you look!
Yes, Sir—those cows do a lot of damage
  to that riparian zone—
It is just loony and a bit strange
  that I have never been able to find a cow
    with a hoof that leaves a track
     like a round rubber tire
    or puts up pie plates and strings paper and cans
     and throws garbage all around
      and then leaves the meadows all torn up!

Spilled Beans and the Orange Swim Suit

The renegade cattle had been gathered
  out of the timber and
  out of the brush,
   and headed down the divide
    over a Forest Service road—
Down towards that forbidden "Riparian" Heaven and
  the tourists' campgrounds—
   headed eventually for timberline
But they had not done all the damage possible
  and there was still a flick of the renegade's tail
   as suddenly they split
  and some wild-eyed cows peeled off
   on a campground road.
The cowgirls split and one followed suit
  on her high jumping Arab
   half broke and full of it.
The dogs were kie-yieing after those long legged calves
  that even a race horse couldn't catch.
And then, of all things,
  there was a camper pulled into a spot—
   all protected, he thought
    from any and all wild things
     by a steep mountain face on the west
     and a wild running creek every other place.

Seconds after the cowgirl yelled—"Watch out!"
  those longhorns hit camp.
    The doors on the pickup and camper all slammed shut
      and it began to shake and rock like an earthquake
        had just hit!
  And you know—I still do not know for sure,
    even to this day—
        if the campers' hearts were really
          beating that hard—
      or if an old mossyback had hit the outfit,
      as she squeezed between them
        and the mountainside.
The cowgirl's horse detested campgrounds
  so she socked the spurs to his hide
    and he cleared a row of brush,
      only to land in the middle of camp!
        right beside the table, all set for supper.
The baked beans could be smelled
  and the steak was still sizzling
    as her dirty old boot dragged across it all
  and then could be heard the
    terrible tinkling and tumbling
      of all the fine camper's china
  as it cascaded to landing amid lemonade,
    beans and tame beef.
Next jump took the bronco through the fire ring
  and into the partially erected tent—
The fire was sent flying and tent pegs a-frying
    as the high flying Arab leaped back towards
      the pickup's new paint job.
And wouldn't you know it—
  but those big rowled spurs
    made the neatest tracks
      that's ever been seen
        in any new paint scene!
The ashen-faced campers all crammed in
  were shaking like the aspen leaf
    as those wild eyed critters
      all swept by—cleaning camp as they went!
As the stampede swept back out on the road and
  towards a cut
    Here came Grandad on his bike
      and would you believe, he was racing

toward that herd!
　　Trying to beat them to the road cut and camp!
Cattle were milling around the unwilling Grandpa
　　and he was shook to his very boot roots!
　　　　But with the pop of the whip
　　　　　　and the nip of a blue heeler
　　　　　　　　the cows sped on to their destiny.
Just up the trail were fifty more head
　　waiting in the wings
　　　　but across that fateful creek
　　one cowgirl peeled off and gave chase
　　　　in the log slash—rough going at its best!
　　Around and around they chased
　　　　until finally they all hit out for—you guessed it—
　　　　　　on a skid road towards that wrecked camp!
As the thundering herd made the last J-hook bend
　　to hit the logging truck ford
　　　　next to that wrecked camp
　　　　　　none would budge into the water,
　　　　　　　　even with whip and heelers biting.
And no wonder, as knee deep in the creek
　　was a two-ton tilly done up
　　　　in a flaming orange bathing suit
　　　　　　that was bulging here and pushing there.
　　She had gotten upstream into a pool
　　　　by the time the dogs got the cows on the move!
Then one old cow decided that orange apparition
　　needed to be put out of the cool water!
　　　　The cowgirl jumped her Arab
　　　　　　off a cutbank
　　　　　　　　to head that cantankerous old rip!
The waves would have sunk the Titanic
　　and the language from that Orange Blimp was gigantic.
As the gutsy Arab turned that snorty old cow
　　back into the herd
　　　　He jumped like he had been shot
　　　　　　and out from behind a large Yellow Pine
　　　　　　　　stepped one-ton tilly—in a Blue Bird sunsuit!
Her suit was not waterproof
　　and all that spooked leap
　　　　sent plenty of liquid spoof
　　　　　　onto that Blue Bird heap

172

As the herd came up out of the rushing stream
    The cowgirl noticed the wrecked camp had come to life!
    The menfolk were hanging out the camper
        and hubby was holding onto the pickup door
        with one hand
            and parting the brush with the other
            never offering to help.
He seemed to just want to know how his women folk went!

The Hip Pie Chainsaw

Now as anyone can tell you
    those wild mountain cattle
        and chain saws just don't get along!

The two cowgirls had fifty pairs strung out
    on an old log road
        easing them up the mountainside.
Suddenly, out of nowhere, it seemed,
    The ugly snarl of a chain saw echoed
        and those wild mountain cattle
            split the drive right then and there!
                with the gals right on their heels.
Dodge that big old yeller pine
    crash through the hawthorn patch
        jump that pile of log slash
            let the tears run in a stream from your eye
                where the stiff spined spruce
                swatted your eyeball!
        Let it all hang out
            chasing those wild, crazed critters
                on a mountainside fit only for
                    mountain goats or—
                        Hippie Woodcutters!
        For the snarly saw was hippie powered.
This sweet, little ol' cowgirl
    politely asked
        the long haired woodcutter to
            "Please, shut your saw off 'till we get by you!"
    and the only answer was
        a nasty grin and hit the throttle full bore.
    Now that steed the cowgirl was on
        didn't like the whine any better than

those longhorns had.
With one bolt—
that big, bold buckskin was moving—
and so was that sweet, little ol' gal's whip!
The next thing that hippie heard
was not the harps of heaven
But a cannon-like shot in his ear
And my-oh-my
suddenly one whole side of his face
was cleaner shaven,
and those stringy, dirty locks
were almost logger length!
And the big, bad buckskin just kept moving on
into the sunset
with that sweet little ol' cowgirl
grinning from ear to ear!

UFOs and White Flags

One early morning a camper heard a terrible noise
down by his favorite fishin' hole.
The cowgirls had struck again.
Those riparian cows just HAD to begin the long journey
As they clattered through the rocks and water
Scattering his illicit chum in his favorite hole.
His little lap dog was furiously
barking in camp.
By then the bunch of wild ones were upon his camp
and because of his little dog
the herd split and one bunch
headed for the biggest opening—
between the camper pickup and his tent.
The camper scooped up his toddler
kicked his dog
and inhaled as hard and long as he could
to let the wild ones run close under his belly!
The ole lead cow had long, sharp horns
and bloodshot eyes
and a crooked mind!
As she bee-lined for that opening
the little hot-dog came to life in a frenzy of action
That ole cow turned left to hook the mutt

he ran under a line between two spruce
and she snagged a line full of diapers,
instead of the dog.
Startled—she jumped to the east to make her escape
and she ran head-on into a line hanging fast and full
of pots and pans!
Now don't think that was not a stampede deluxe!
with the old renegade at the helm
flying her flags from each polished horn!
It would not have taken a Girl Scout
to follow the carnage!
For a hawthorn snagged a diaper on the fly—
a skillet blazed a fir–in non-regulation style!
A pan floated down the stream like a drunken ship
and a kettle had its metal tested
as the stampede stomped it into the bank!
Two diapers were left looking for a home on a
service berry bush—
and fluttering over the remains
of the bent-up aluminum at the base of the pine!
There were even diapers on a skid road—
so the cat skinners wouldn't get lost!
and one last pot went into orbit—
Maybe that is what that crazed camper down the creek
saw that night
and thought he had a UFO
with a white flag at full mast.

Senior Citizens Picnic

Two seasoned citizens had spent
a beautiful day on the creek
and came supper time
they set about to dine
on a blanket in an island's clover.
The peace and quiet was shattered up the creek
by two cowgirls digging renegade cows
out of the Riparian zone and hawthorn
But the noise was of no worry to them
on their isolated island, until—
A large black charger came thundering
right down the middle of the creek
knee deep water splashing out everywhere!

There were cows bellering, dogs heeling, cowgirls muttering
    albeit, rather loudly
        all in the cool streambed
    But still they felt safe
        all tucked in behind their walls of willow.
The cattle changed directions and headed west
      The cowgirl on the Big Black Charger was doing her best
        To head the rest on down the creek a ways.

Spurs all wet and shiny
    The Black all charged up to go
        They came up out of the deep water like a phantom
      Onto the island they leaped, amidst a great spray
        of rainbow hued water.
The landing was anything but welcome
      for on that island was the Senior Citizens' picnic
        and the blanket spread out between them was loaded
           with goodies.
The big Black Charger landed fair and square
      in the middle of that blanket—water a-flying!
      The blue heelers were right alongside
        and made a mighty fine supper
           as they inhaled any and all the goodies
             that survived
               the four steel horseshoes!
The cowgirl never stopped to pass the time of day
    or to see if there were any cardiac problems
      As she had enough of her own—
          never knowing anyone, was around, anywhere
           until that eventful Blanket Landing!

That Ol' Strawberry Roan
(Leaving Home)

Her parents were both wild horses
Running free and wild out in the Owyhee.
      They were running into a dog food can
        And she was put on a bottle and spoiled rotten.
Six years down the road,
  Her adopted family was fed up
  With her tricks and no treats
And much to the relief of both her family and farrier—

A cowgirl hauled the old rip to the mountains.
  The family was so glad to see her go
    They even insisted on throwing in a gunny sack
      Full of cackling chickens up in the truck's overhang.
Now that cowgirl should have had second thoughts about then!
  After all—there were no tears shed by family
  And the chickens were plumb healthy
    They even offered to send a kid along to help for awhile!
As the air got thinner and cooler
And the mountain steeper and the road rougher.
  She seemed to take on new life!
    Nuzzle the sack full of chicken to see if they are still
      kickin'
    Bite the dog's hind leg
    Play chicken with the heeler—nose to nose in the
      overhang.
    Kick the tail-gate to splinters
    Strike at the unlucky dog that fell
      Out of the overhang while playing chicken
      While sitting on a sack of squawking fowls
    Dance and prance to the rope's end
      And make the truck sway like a camel in a
        hurricane!
Finally in desperation
  The cowgirl drove in under an overhanging pine
  And a good swat on the steel bed and horse
      heads with a branch
  Filled with heavy, wet pine cones—
    Helped settle things down real fast.
      Even the chickens quit squalling!

Horse Trampolines and Cows

This ol' roan was renamed "Ginger"
  As she was just full of it—and many and varied
    Were her escapades to be
      In the few short years allotted
        To this Demon in Horseflesh!
She could and would walk on her hindlegs—rider and all
  Till one might wonder if maybe she
      Had some of that "fur-in" blood in her from Austria.
But jumping was not her forte
  Unless propelled by a horse sized trampoline

Her maiden voyage after cows
    Was over a long, log bridge
        Spanning a raging river in spring runoff.
She was fooled into going over the first time
    But when the cows came back towards her
        And the other cowgirl yelled—"Turn those suckers!"
           All the gal on "Ginger" could do was yell
        Something incoherent in between the bucks
          And the dancing on Hind Legs.
By the time the cows got to the bridge
    She was dancing on the east side of the log span
        Her rider hanging on for dear life
           Up over, and dangling out over, the raging flood
           below her.
In desperation, the cowgirl socked her spurs home
    And that ol' red roan lit out for home
        In one great leap!
She landed in the middle of that forty foot span
    And the bridge buckled and bucked and then sprung
        Like a giant equine trampoline!
Ginger and her wild-eyed cowgirl went flying
    Off that log trampoline
        Like they were headed for the Last Great Roundup
        in the Sky!
As luck would have it—
    They both landed twenty feet away and on the west end
        Of that log contraption
          Which was still buckling and heaving
        Over that wild torrent of snowmelt!
Sock the spurs to her again
    And over and under her a little
        With that rawhide romal
          And maybe by the time retirement rolls around—
           The "Ol' Strawberry Roan" will be broke to ride!

Dancing Slippers and Spurs
A Farrier's Ballet

This old red roan had never been shod standing—
    The bear of a farrier had always thrown her
        Cause she'd fight like a holy terror.
The cowgirl said that was for the birds

give this ol' nag an education!
:flection—it was probably a draw
r of the "Ol' Strawberry Roan"!
on learned the ropes like how to
egs and still reach around and
wgirl farrier's lumbar.
e a kicking fit
vith only three nails
 go into orbit.
ed a back fetlock
ong lariat
ick against it in an ankle lock.
:ick—
g and then the other
ith both hind feet
ading towards the moon.
.n she would start it all over again.
ne stopped for some oxygen
A quick flip of the lariat
Would start the show again
If the ol' gal decided she'd had enough
For a spell
Then the cowgirl would step in real close
And pick up that unregistered lethal weapon
Via the rope and start to rasp!
On this horse—a cowboy fit was plenty good 'nuff!
If the dancing slipper touched on three points of hoof—
Why you just spit eight nails at it real fast!
And jumped back in a scurry of dust
Cause she was sure to be in a hurry
to leave the scene!
Many's the time she rolled her buggered up cowgirl farrier.
And gave her a dust bath in that old corral of torture.
One day the cowgirl went rolling southeast
And her hammer flew due north
Through a plank fence and beyond
Never to be found for many a month!
But she could be lethal while she had her cowgirl
Bent over double working on her front hoof.
She would look around to see what she could see!
And then while standing on just two legs
Quickly kick the Stetson off the farrier's head
And trample it into the dust and manure.

That was some farrier's ballet!

Bill and Sally

One fine Fourth of July
    Bill and Sally parked their pickup camper
        With their name plainly painted on the end
            Upon a knoll, overlooking a rushing river.
      This idyllic scene was right on the "Cowgirl Freeway"
        And what a sight to behold—as the holiday unfolded!
First it was Sally, on a cool sunrise
    In a tent-like muu-muu
        Floating in the morning mist
            In and out of the timber
                Like some long-ago ghost.
Then the sun took command
    And when the cowgirls rode back towards the home corrals
        There sat Sally, in all her glory
            Squeezed into a skimpy black swimsuit—
                roll upon roll!
        Reveling in all that solar energy.
That evening as the cowgirls rode by again—
    Sally was a vivid study in black and red
        And it was pretty evident—
            If Sally was going to wear anything else
        But that skimpy black suit for the next three
            days of celebrating
      It would have to be in the flowing, flowered muu-muu!
The second day Sally gave up on the muu-muu in the heat
    And would you believe—she was sun worshiping again—
        This time with black glasses to match her suit
            But nothing vivid enough to match her skin!
        By eve, when the cowgirls were riding home
            It looked as if Sally's wrinkles were sunburned—
                Even to their very depths!
The third day—it was overcast
    And Sally thought she would not be an outcast
        If she looked like a large red cherry, cast in black.
            So out to her sunning point
        She shuffled her bright red wrinkles!
The sight was so brilliant and bad
    That the sun completely hid its face behind a cloud.

It just could not take it another day
The sight of Sally simmering and broiling
in that skimpy
Black suit was just too much.
The black cumulus clouds flashed some lightning bolts
towards Sally—
As if in disbelief of what the bolt revealed—
The clouds revolted and dropped some rain
on the scorched Sally—
No doubt hoping it would send her into the camper.
As the cowgirls came sloshing by
In warm clothes and yellow slickers—
Sally was nowhere to be seen.
But up the hill—through the timber—
came a red glow—
Kind of like a sunset in a rainstorm!
When the cowgirls got up to the cattle guard
There in all her miserable glory—was Sally
And you guessed it—too burned to be in anything else—
But that bulging black suit.
And too burned to bend over and pick up firewood.
Husband Bill was loading up crispy Sally
With wet firewood—a sight for sore eyes!
Even in the rain!
One cowgirl almost rode her horse through the cattle guard
Taking in all the astounding scenery in the downpour!
And her ol' strawberry roan about fell out
Of her new steel shoes
When she peeled that white rimmed eye at
The apparition in black and red!

APPENDIX: PEOPLE IN THIS BOOK

DENNIS and JOY WEAVER

Our local friends and neighbors helped a lot to make life nice while we were working on the mountain. They were friendly, helpful and generous. Dennis and Joy Weaver lived about seven miles from us. He was a long-haul truck driver and could weld anything. I think he could weld your knee joint back together! If I came down with a piece broken on the truck, or the tractor, or a pickup, or a pack saddle, he would stop whatever he was doing and fix our problem. We were always welcome to use their phone. Then they would insist that we eat ice cream and cookies.

BOB and DOTTY HARTGROVE

Bob and Dotty Hartgrove were also long-haul truck driving neighbors. They didn't have electricity, either, but he had a shop in Ola for awhile and would fix things for us there sometimes. If our pickup battery was dead and needed a jump, he was always willing to help.

One day Bev and I were out working in Third Fork pocket. We had dug cows out of the brush and were late getting them up off the creek. It was hot. About eleven o'clock we got up on the road, and here came a little blue jeep. We both knew instantly it was Weavers' jeep. Here were Joy and Dotty bringing us cold pop and the works, right out there in the middle of nowhere. I told them they were the best ride-in drive-in I had ever seen. They could have sold that stuff for a fancy price!

Another year while we were working on cow camp fences, along came Dotty with Mary Dudley and a hot rhubarb pie, delivered right out there on the fence line. That was good, I'll tell you.

BUCK and JESSIE CHERRY

Down in the Emmett Valley was a special couple, Buck and Jesse Cherry. She was retired from school teaching. I had become acquainted with Buck years earlier when he was the foreman of a crew building the Loop Road, and I was on the crew. He always had a twinkle in his eye and had a joke ready.

Buck looked out for me. One day I was working on that road. Buck said, "Carol, that old dog of yours is getting pretty tired. I think we better stop here in the shade and let him rest." He knew it was *me* getting hot and tired. He was like a second father to me.

Buck passed away, and Jessie eventually married Dr. Ralph Goodwin. She was always generous and thoughtful. Sometimes when we rode down off the mountain, Jessie would be waiting for us with the barbecue going, ready to put the steak on. She would bring everything for supper, and we ate as soon as we got there. She would bring me ice cold root beer to pour on the ice cream she brought to go with the huckleberry pie.

ORVILLE and ALOISIA HARRIS

Orville and Aloisia Harris were Emmett people. They had been riders as a young married couple for Ola C and other places. They also worked in mining. Eloise cooked in the mining camps, and was a great cook. Orville got a job with Idaho Power. After he retired he had extra time on his hands, and he would show us horseshoeing tricks we didn't know existed. They introduced us to Doc Hyde.

DOC NORRIS HYDE

Doc was a veterinarian and a once-in-a-lifetime acquaintance. He always had a ready joke and a twinkle in his eye, and rode in the fall for us the last two years. His wife Norma was knowledgeable and intellectual, but got in on all his jokes, rode over the mountain with him and his Redbone hounds, and kept him in line.

WE HOPE YOU ENJOY THE RIDE
ALONG WITH BEV + I AS WE
CHASE WILD CATTLE ON IDAHO's
WEST MOUNTAIN. IT's CHAPS LARD'N
FUN!

Carol Shelter

OLA, IDAHO

RIDIN' *Bev Martin*

The
MOUNTAIN

$$\frac{671}{1590}$$